Co<

MW01062350

Turfgrass
Problems

Picture Clues and
Management Options

By

Eva Gussack
Extension Associate
Department of Horticulture
Cornell University

Frank S. Rossi, Ph.D.
Assistant Professor of Turfgrass Science
New York State Extension Turfgrass Specialist
Department of Horticulture
Cornell University

Natural Resource, Agriculture, and
Engineering Service (NRAES)
Cooperative Extension • PO Box 4557
Ithaca, New York 14852-4557

NRAES–125
June 2001

ISBN-13: 978-0-935817-62-1

ISBN-10: 0-935817-62-X

Library of Congress Cataloging-in-Publication Data

Gussack, Eva, 1956-
  Turfgrass problems: picture clues and management options / Eva Gussack, Frank S. Rossi.
      p. cm. -- (NRAES ; 125)
  Includes bibliographical references.
  ISBN 0-935817-62-X (pbk.)
    1. Turfgrasses--Diseases and pests. 2. Weeds--Identification. 3. Turf management. I. Rossi, Frank S., 1962- II. Title. III. NRAES (Series) ; 125

SB608.T87 G87 2001
635.9'6429--dc21

                                                                00-068111

Requests to reprint parts of this book should be sent to NRAES. In your request, please state which parts of the book you would like to reprint and describe how you intend to use the reprinted material. Contact NRAES if you have any questions.

Natural Resource, Agriculture, and Engineering Service (NRAES)
Cooperative Extension • PO Box 4557
Ithaca, New York 14852-4557
Phone: (607) 255-7654 • Fax: (607) 254-8770
E-mail: NRAES@CORNELL.EDU
Web site: WWW.NRAES.ORG

Contents

Acknowledgments

This book was inspired by *Picture Clues to Turfgrass Problems,* which was published by Cornell Cooperative Extension in 1982 and written by A. Martin Petrovic, Maria T. Cinque, Richard W. Smiley, and Haruo Tashiro. The authors of this book would like to acknowledge the importance of *Picture Clues to Turfgrass Problems* to their work here.

The authors are greatly indebted to many people who contributed to this project. The manuscript was peer-reviewed by experts whose comments improved the accuracy, clarity, and usefulness of the final product. See pages 201–202 for a list of peer reviewers. Thanks to Rose Harmon, Paul Robbins, Mike Villani, and Leslie Weston—all of Cornell University—for providing text used in this book. Thanks also to the individuals, organizations, and universities who generously contributed many of the photos. See pages 203–204 for a list of photo credits.

Thanks to The Art Department in Ithaca, New York, for drawing the raster patterns in chapter 5. Thanks to Jim Houghton of The Graphic Touch, also in Ithaca, for illustrating the sampling procedures in chapter 2.

Jeff Popow, NRAES managing editor, coordinated the peer review of the manuscript, ensured the quality of the photograph processing, and managed the overall project. Cathleen Walker, NRAES production editor, copyedited the book, managed the development of illustrations, and gathered photograph permissions. Jeff and Cathleen collaborated on the design.

How to Use This Guide

About This Guide

Turfgrass is used for lawns, golf courses, sports fields, and in commercial sod production. *Turfgrass Problems: Picture Clues and Management Options* can assist anyone interested in managing turfgrass—from homeowners who have little or no formal training to experienced professionals. The guide covers problems associated with **cool-season turfgrasses**. The principal species of cool-season turfgrasses are creeping bentgrasses, colonial bentgrasses, Kentucky bluegrasses, annual bluegrasses, fine-leaf fescues, tall fescues, and perennial ryegrasses.

This guide does not contain specific chemical control recommendations for the problems that are discussed. For the latest recommendations, consult your local Cooperative Extension office.

The steps outlined below will help you use this guide to zero in on a diagnosis quickly and efficiently. Terms defined in the glossary are in **bold**.

Eliminate Abiotic Problems First

Your turfgrass problem may be **abiotic** (nonliving) and the result of poor growing conditions. If so, the problem can be diagnosed by process of elimination using the picture clues and problem descriptions in chapter 3 (see page 16).

Consult the Timelines: The Gateway to Biotic Problems

If **abiotic** problems can be eliminated, consult the timelines in chapter 1 (see page 4). The timelines are a "gateway" to the picture clues for **biotic** (living) problems—diseases, insects, and weeds. They are a general guide to when a problem might occur in most northern climates and are arranged by the time of year a problem is noticed. The timelines also highlight the pest growth stages that could be causing the problem. For example, insect problems can be caused by the adult insect or by **grubs** and **larvae**. Consulting the timelines before visiting the picture clue chapters will reduce the list of possible problems and facilitate a diagnosis.

To use the timelines, locate the current month and average temperature ranges in your area. This will give you an idea of possible problems. The page numbers listed along the left side of each timeline will help you jump to the picture clues for a review of the problems. There could be several possible diagnoses at first, but a review of the problem descriptions should help narrow the choices.

If you still have two or three possible explanations, try examining the problem closer. Insects can sometimes be identified by observing a **raster pattern** (see pages 112–114), and diseases sometimes exhibit a specific fungal structure. This type of close-up examination requires a hand lens or magnifying glass. A hand lens is also handy for examining characteristics of weeds.

Sample for Further Testing

Turfgrass Problems: Picture Clues and Management Options includes a chapter on the basics of sampling (see chapter 2, page 12). The first step to good sampling is keen observation. Is the problem in a particular location? How does the problem appear from a distance? Is there a pattern to the injury? Is an insect or organism evident upon closer examination?

The sampling chapter provides useful methods for working through a proper diagnosis. For example, it describes techniques that can be used to determine insect problems, such as peeling back the turf to look for **grubs** or using an irritating solution to force insects to the surface.

Don't Give Up!

Even the most experienced diagnosticians have difficulty with problems observed in the field. Don't be discouraged. Collect a sample of the insect, diseased turf, or weed and follow the directions provided in chapter 2 (page 12) for submitting samples to a diagnostic lab or a local Cooperative Extension office.

Step-by-Step Instructions for a Proper Diagnosis

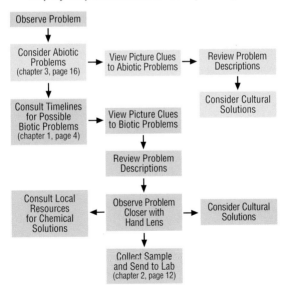

CHAPTER 1

Timelines

Timeline for Disease Symptoms

Page Number	Season / Temperature Range / Month(s) — Disease	Winter <32°F — Jan Feb	Early Spr. 32–60°F — Mar Apr	Late Spr. 61–80°F — May Jun	Summer >80°F — Jul Aug	Early Fall 80–61°F — Sep Mid-Oct	Late Fall 60–32°F — Mid-Oct Nov	Winter <32°F — Dec
	Late Fall to Early Spring							
47	Pink Snow Mold							
50	Typhula Blight/Gray Snow Mold							
	Spring and Fall							
53	Basal Rot Anthracnose							
55	Cool-Season Pythium Root and Crown Rot							
57	Dollar Spot							
59	Fairy Rings							
61	Necrotic Ring Spot							
63	Pink Patch							
65	Powdery Mildew							
67	Red Thread							
69	Spring/Fall Leaf Blight							
72	Spr./Fall Leaf Spots/Melting Out							

Key   High disease potential   Medium disease potential   Low disease potential

Timeline for Disease Symptoms
(continued)

Note: Dates in the timelines are not exact and can vary according to weather conditions and climatic zone. See "How to Use This Guide" on page 1 for guidance in using the timelines.

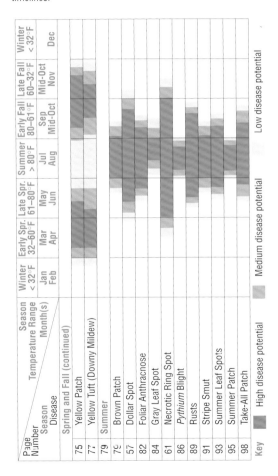

Page Number	Season / Disease	Season Temperature Range Month(s)	Winter <32°F Jan Feb	Early Spr. 32–60°F Mar Apr	Late Spr. 61–80°F May Jun	Summer >80°F Jul Aug	Early Fall 80–61°F Sep Mid-Oct	Late Fall 60–32°F Mid-Oct Nov	Winter <32°F Dec
	Spring and Fall (continued)								
75	Yellow Patch								
77	Yellow Tuft (Downy Mildew)								
	Summer								
79	Brown Patch								
57	Dollar Spot								
82	Foliar Anthracnose								
84	Gray Leaf Spot								
61	Necrotic Ring Spot								
86	*Pythium* Blight								
89	Rusts								
91	Stripe Smut								
93	Summer Leaf Spots								
95	Summer Patch								
98	Take-All Patch								

Key: ■ High disease potential ▨ Medium disease potential □ Low disease potential

Timeline for Insects

Note: Dates in the timelines are not exact and can vary according to weather conditions and climatic zone. See "How to Use This Guide" on page 1 for guidance in using the timelines.

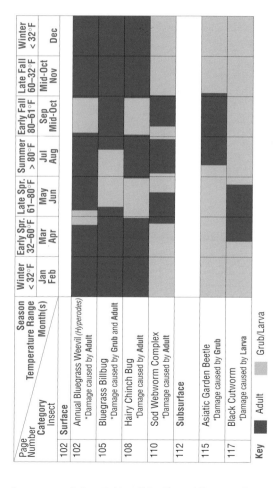

Page Number	Category Insect	Winter < 32°F Jan Feb	Early Spr. 32–60°F Mar Apr	Late Spr. 61–80°F May Jun	Summer > 80°F Jul Aug	Early Fall 80–61°F Sep Mid-Oct	Late Fall 60–32°F Mid-Oct Nov	Winter < 32°F Dec
	Season **Temperature Range** **Month(s)**							
102	**Surface**							
102	Annual Bluegrass Weevil *(Hyperodes)* *Damage caused by **Adult**							
105	Bluegrass Billbug *Damage caused by **Grub and Adult**							
108	Hairy Chinch Bug *Damage caused by **Adult**							
110	Sod Webworm Complex *Damage caused by **Adult**							
112	**Subsurface**							
115	Asiatic Garden Beetle *Damage caused by **Grub**							
117	Black Cutworm *Damage caused by **Larva**							

Key: ■ Adult ▨ Grub/Larva

Timeline for Insects (continued)

Note: Dates in the timelines are not exact and can vary according to weather conditions and climatic zone. See "How to Use This Guide" on page 1 for guidance in using the timelines.

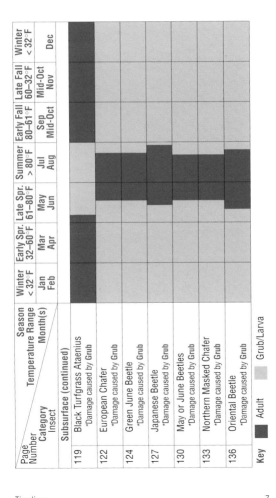

Page Number	Category Insect	Winter < 32°F Jan Feb	Early Spr. 32–60°F Mar Apr	Late Spr. 61–80°F May Jun	Summer > 80°F Jul Aug	Early Fall 80–61°F Sep Mid-Oct	Late Fall 60–32°F Mid-Oct Nov	Winter < 32°F Dec
	Subsurface (continued)							
119	Black Turfgrass Ataenius *Damage caused by Grub							
122	European Chafer *Damage caused by Grub							
124	Green June Beetle *Damage caused by Grub							
127	Japanese Beetle *Damage caused by Grub							
130	May or June Beetles *Damage caused by Grub							
133	Northern Masked Chafer *Damage caused by Grub							
136	Oriental Beetle *Damage caused by Grub							

Key   ■ Adult   ▢ Grub/Larva

Timeline for Weeds

Note: Dates in the timelines are not exact and can vary according to weather conditions and climatic zone. See "How to Use This Guide" on page 1 for guidance in using the timelines.

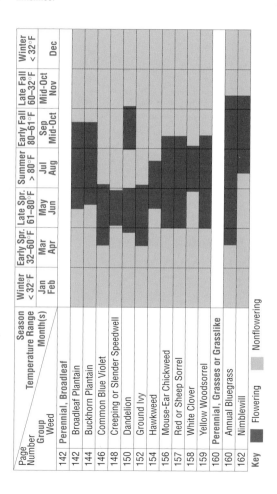

Page Number	Group Weed	Season Temperature Range Month(s)	Winter < 32°F Jan Feb	Early Spr. 32–60°F Mar Apr	Late Spr. 61–80°F May Jun	Summer > 80°F Jul Aug	Early Fall 80–61°F Sep Mid-Oct	Late Fall 60–32°F Mid-Oct Nov	Winter < 32°F Dec
142	**Perennial, Broadleaf**								
142	Broadleaf Plantain								
144	Buckhorn Plantain								
146	Common Blue Violet								
148	Creeping or Slender Speedwell								
150	Dandelion								
152	Ground Ivy								
154	Hawkweed								
156	Mouse-Ear Chickweed								
157	Red or Sheep Sorrel								
158	White Clover								
159	Yellow Woodsorrel								
160	**Perennial, Grasses or Grasslike**								
160	Annual Bluegrass								
162	Nimblewill								

Key: ▓ Flowering ░ Nonflowering

Timeline for Weeds (continued)

Note: Dates in the timelines are not exact and can vary according to weather conditions and climatic zone. See "How to Use This Guide" on page 1 for guidance in using the timelines.

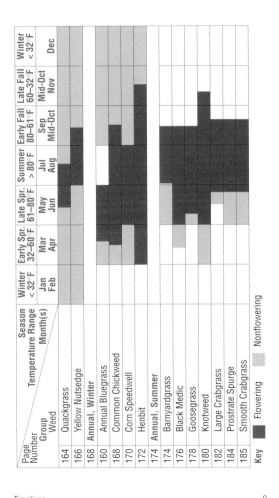

Page Number	Group Weed	Season Temperature Range Month(s)	Winter <32°F Jan Feb	Early Spr. 32–60°F Mar Apr	Late Spr. 61–80°F May Jun	Summer >80°F Jul Aug	Early Fall 80–61°F Sep Mid-Oct	Late Fall 60–32°F Mid-Oct Nov	Winter <32°F Dec
164	Quackgrass								
166	Yellow Nutsedge								
168	Annual, Winter								
160	Annual Bluegrass								
168	Common Chickweed								
170	Corn Speedwell								
172	Henbit								
174	Annual, Summer								
174	Barnyardgrass								
176	Black Medic								
178	Goosegrass								
180	Knotweed								
182	Large Crabgrass								
184	Prostrate Spurge								
185	Smooth Crabgrass								

Key: Flowering   Nonflowering

Growing Degree Days — Refining the Timelines

The authors created the timelines in this guide to provide a simple starting point for diagnosing turfgrass problems. While the timelines provide a *general* guide to when a problem might occur in most northern climates, they are predicated on historical weather data that assumes average temperatures and rainfall. If current weather conditions at your location are not average, there may be significant variability in the timelines.

Living things such as turfgrass plants, weeds, insects, and pathogens do not mature in response to specific calendar dates (except for some plants that flower in response to a certain daylength and light intensity that does coincide with a calendar date). In general, as temperature increases throughout a season, plants and insects actively develop in response to the heat.

Biologists have developed a method known as **growing degree days (GDD)** to monitor temperatures that coincide with plant or insect growth. GDD are a measure of accumulated heat units relative to a predetermined base temperature (see example calculation on page 11). However, little research has been done to correlate GDD with turfgrass problems; therefore, you will not find reference to GDD in the descriptions in this book.

The benefit of monitoring turfgrass problems based on GDD is that you can add precision to the diagnostic process. By regularly monitoring GDD, you can create a "local" timeline based on actual conditions. You will be able to develop your own historical database of GDD and timelines that better coincide with your turfgrass problems.

Example Calculation of Growing Degree Days

Growing degree days (GDD) measure heat units accumulated over time relative to a base temperature. They can be used to monitor the developmental status of plants and insects, as plant and insect development is temperature-dependent: Each species must reach a certain base temperature to begin development and accumulate a certain number of "heat units" to reach maturity. Measuring maturity with GDD is more accurate than using the calendar date, as GDD take into account actual temperatures, which vary from year to year.

The formula below can be used to calculate daily GDD. For many northern turf problems, a base temperature of 50°F (10°C) can be used.

GDD = Average daily temperature − Base temperature

For example, on a day with a high temperature of 65°F and a low temperature of 45°F, five GDD would be accumulated:

GDD = [(65 + 45) ÷ 2] − 50 = 55 − 50 = 5 GDD

The chart below shows GDD accumulated over a week in April. Note that if the GDD calculation results in a negative number, the GDD accumulated for that day is zero.

Calendar date:	4/1	4/2	4/3	4/4	4/5	4/6	4/7
Daily average temperature (°F):	55	65	63	50	48	60	70
Base temperature (°F):	50	50	50	50	50	50	50
Daily GDD:	5	15	13	0	0	10	20
Cumulative GDD:	5	20	33	33	33	43	63

In the example above, 63 GDD were accumulated during the first week in April. GDD can be continually calculated and tallied to monitor the developmental status of a plant or insect species relative to GDD throughout the growing season.

CHAPTER 2

On-Site Sampling Procedures for Successful Problem Solving

Note: Terms defined in the glossary are in **bold** throughout this chapter.

There is no substitute for regular site monitoring in developing a trained eye and realizing turfgrass problems early on. A successful diagnosis depends on following logical steps to gather enough evidence to support or exclude potential causal agents. Listed below are some steps to follow for diagnosing and taking samples of problems.

1. Know the general soil conditions, the turfgrass species, and, if possible, the turfgrass **cultivar**. Certain pests are specific to a species or cultivar or related to specific soil conditions, such as high **pH** or moisture status.

2. Consult the timelines supplied in this guide (see chapter 1, page 4) to see what pests could be active.

3. Know the prevailing weather conditions as well as **growing degree days (GDD)** for the current growing season. GDD are used to

quantify the accumulation of heat units during a growing season. They can be used as a guide for **scouting**, since plant and pest development may not always coincide with the calendar date. See pages 10–11 for more information about GDD and a sample calculation. Soil temperature (especially in spring) can also be used to monitor certain weeds and insects.

4. Observe the problem from a distance to identify features like high, dry areas or low areas with water or drainage problems. Circular, patchy, **blighted**, or diffuse areas may also be characteristic of a problem.

5. Use a hand lens or magnifying glass to observe individual plants and plant parts. Look for clues such as the presence of fungal structures or insects on or around the plants, the shape of leaf **lesions**, roots that are deformed or discolored, and wilting.

6. Sample insect populations using one or more of the following methods:
   • Disclosing solution (figure 1.1, page 14): Add 2 tablespoons of liquid dish detergent to 1 gallon of water. Pour the solution over 1 square yard of **turf**. Cutworms, web-worms, billbugs, and earthworms will come to the surface.
   • Flotation (figure 1.2, page 14): Cut both ends out of a large coffee can. Drive the can 2–3 inches into the ground. Add several inches of water until the turf is submerged. After 20–30 minutes, chinch bug adults and **nymphs** will float to the surface and can be counted.

Figure 1.1
Using a disclosing solution to sample insect populations.

The solution is poured over 1 square yard of turf.

Figure 1.2
Using flotation to sample insect populations.

- Soil examination (figure 1.3): Cut three sides of a 1-square-foot turf area with a shovel. Peel back the sod layer to expose **grubs** and billbug **larvae**.
- **Cup cutter**: Take a cup cutter to a depth of 4 inches and examine the resulting sample for grubs. Note: A cup cutter sample is 0.1 square foot.

7. Use a hand lens to examine the **raster pattern** on any grubs to help identify the species. The raster pattern is the arrangement of hairs or spines on the bottom end of the

Figure 1.3
Using soil
examination to
sample insect
populations.

Remove about
1 square yard of turf.

grub by the anal slit (see chapter 5, pages 112–114, for more information).

8. If no insects are evident and weeds are not a problem, look at diseases (chapter 4) or **abiotic** problems (chapter 3) and attempt a diagnosis. Compare your findings with the text and photos supplied in this guide.

9. If you still cannot make a positive diagnosis, collect samples and submit them to a diagnostic lab. If you suspect a disease, take samples from an area that includes both the actively growing and unhealthy turfgrass, wrap them in moist paper towels or newspaper (not plastic), and send them by an overnight service to ensure freshness. Package weed samples in the same manner, and send insects in a container. You need to be the eyes for the diagnostician. It is critical that you include the grass species, a description of overall and close-up symptoms, cultural practices in use, weather conditions, and notes about any pesticides or fertilizers applied before and during the onset of symptoms.

10. Maintain detailed site records to develop a turf management history that will help you anticipate and solve future problems.

CHAPTER 3
Abiotic Problems

The term **abiotic** means nonliving. Problems categorized as abiotic are not caused by living organisms, such as weeds or insects, but by "nonliving" factors, such as weather, poor soil conditions, improper moisture or nutrient levels, misuse of chemicals, and improper use of turfgrass maintenance equipment.

The discussion for each problem in this chapter is divided into three sections. The Appearance section describes how the problem will be noticeable to the turfgrass manager. The Problem Description section describes where the problem commonly occurs, what may have caused the problem, and what the consequences of the problem are on turfgrass health. Finally, the Cultural Options section lists possible methods for correcting the problem and ways to avoid the problem in the future.

Terms defined in the glossary are in **bold** throughout this chapter (see **abiotic** above).

Contents: Abiotic Problems

▼ Black Layer

Photo 3.1   Black layer.
Anaerobic conditions result in black layer (arrow).

Photo 3.2   Layered soil.
Note layers (arrows).

Appearance
- Yellow to brown areas that have thin **turf** in irregular patterns

Problem Description
- Usually a problem on putting greens with a high sand content
- Occurs when sands are layered over heavier soils, creating a perched water table
- Soils become **anaerobic** (have a low oxygen content); black layers can have a rotten egg odor (photo 3.1)
- Sampling the soil profile will reveal well-defined layering (photo 3.2)

Cultural Options
- Improve surface and subsurface drainage
- Use **core aeration** and backfill with sand to improve gas exchange and enhance root development
- Use **topdressing** materials with physical characteristics similar to existing root zone
- Avoid irrigation waters with a high **pH**

▼ Compaction

Photo 3.3   Bare area caused by compaction from high traffic.

Photo 3.4   Thin turf caused by compaction.

▼ Compaction
(continued)

Appearance

- Bare areas or browning or low-quality, thin **turf** areas that are the first to green up in the spring (photos 3.3 and 3.4)
- Area is invaded with both **annual** grasses and broadleaf weeds

Problem Description

- Occurs on heavily trafficked areas (photo 3.3), especially on soils having a high clay content
- Root growth is restricted
- Plants are more susceptible to temperature, drought, and disease stresses
- It is difficult to insert a probe or knife into the turf

Cultural Options

- **Core cultivation**; ideally, remove plugs and **topdress** with a coarse-textured material to increase porosity
- **Renovation**
- Use compaction-tolerant species such as **perennial** ryegrasses

▼ Dog Spots and Salts

Photo 3.5 Dog spot (arrows).

Photo 3.6 Salt injury.
Damage associated with road salting.

▼ Dog Spots and Salts
(continued)

Appearance

- Dog spots appear in circular patches of scorched, dead **turf**
- Dog spots will often have a margin of dark green grass surrounding the dead turf (photo 3.5)
- Salt damage appears as irregular, scorched patches by roadways and sidewalks (photo 3.6)

Problem Description

- Concentrated **soluble** salts reach toxic levels in the soil

Cultural Options

- Flush area with water immediately after dog urinates to wash leaves
- **Leach** salts from soil by drenching with water
- Fence dogs away from area
- Train dog to urinate in nonturf areas

▼ Drought

Photo 3.7   Early drought.
Note lightly browning turf at right edge and top of photo.

Photo 3.8   Advanced drought.
Turf is straw-colored. Note that higher-mowed turf is less stressed (arrow).

▼ Drought
(continued)

Appearance

- Plants appear bluish green when wilted and progress to straw-colored (photos 3.7 and 3.8)
- Wheel marks and footprints persist

Problem Description

- Higher-mowed **turf** is less stressed (photo 3.8)
- Symptoms may first appear along sidewalks, roads, buildings, and tops of slopes
- A probe inserted in the soil indicates dryness
- Problem is more severe in dry, powdery soils on shallow and compacted areas
- Problem is easily confused with root-feeding insects such as sod webworm (see page 110), billbugs (see page 105), and white **grubs** (see pages 112–114)

Cultural Options

- Delay onset of drought by increasing mowing height
- Look beneath the turf surface to eliminate the possibility of insects
- Consider **cultivation** for layered soils
- Consider **wetting agents** for soils and **thatch** that are difficult to wet

▼ Dull Mower Leaf Blade Injury

Photo 3.9   Dull mower leaf blade injury.
Note shredded blades.

Appearance

- **Turf** will appear gray after mowing and have a straw brown appearance within a few days
- Under close observation, leaf tips will be torn and shredded (photo 3.9)

Problem Description

- Common on areas with a high percentage of ryegrass and tall fescues
- Injury can make plant more susceptible to disease and increase water loss

Cultural Options

- Keep mower blades sharpened and equipment properly adjusted
- Avoid mowing when grass leaves are wet or experiencing moisture stress

▼ Fertilizer Burns

University of Nebraska

Photo 3.10   Fertilizer burns (arrow).

Appearance
- Stripes of dark green, white, or brown **turf** follow fertilizer application route (photo 3.10)
- **Foliar** burn appears rapidly in one to two days

Problem Description
- Highly **soluble** sources of nitrogen (N) can burn, especially when applied in hot, dry conditions

Cultural Options
- Water-in highly soluble N sources to prevent burn
- Apply fertilizer evenly and make sure equipment is properly calibrated to deliver the proper amount
- Avoid high percentages of water-soluble N at high temperatures; use slow-release N sources when temperatures are above 80°F (27°C)

▼ Frost Damage

Photo 3.11   Frost damage (from a distance).
Note white frost in low, shaded area.

Rossi

Photo 3.12   Damage associated with foot traffic on frosted turf.

University of Nebraska

▼ Frost Damage
(continued)

Appearance
- Initially water-soaked **turf** turns straw brown; becomes matted; and maintains imprints of tire marks, shoe prints, or animal tracks (photos 3.11 and 3.12)

Problem Description
- Ice within the plant melts rapidly with pressure from foot or tire traffic, resulting in ruptured cell membranes

Cultural Options
- Do not allow traffic on turf until frost subsides
- **Syringe** to eliminate frost
- Apply **wetting agents** to reduce **dew** formation

▼ Ice Damage

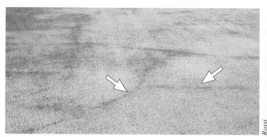

Photo 3.13   Ice damage.
Note cracks in ice (arrows).

Appearance

- Green, irregular strips where ice cracked are interspersed within water-soaked, matted **turf** (photo 3.13)

Problem Description

- Prolonged ice cover suffocates the plants underneath
- Common on compacted soils with poor surface drainage and in low-lying areas

Cultural Options

- Reduce **compaction** throughout the season
- Improve surface and subsurface drainage
- Physically break up the ice sheets after 45–60 days on annual bluegrass and **perennial** ryegrass
- Apply a light **topdressing** of a darkening agent (**compost** or **organic fertilizers**) to absorb heat and create pores in the ice

▼ Localized Dry Spots

Photo 3.14   Localized dry spots.
Note brownish areas that lack morning dew.

Appearance

- Irregular patches of stressed or dead **turf** (photo 3.14)

Problem Description

- Localized dry spot is caused by water-repellant (**hydrophobic**) soils
- Problem associated with excessive **thatch** (see page 42); **compaction** (see page 20); high, dry spots; and sometimes fairy rings (see page 59)

Cultural Options

- Maintain adequate fertility
- Maintain thatch at less than 0.5 inch
- **Aerate** to alleviate compaction and enhance rooting
- In severe cases, use a commercially available **wetting agent**

▼ Moss and Algae

Photo 3.15   Moss (from a distance).

Photo 3.16   Moss (close-up).

Photo 3.17   Algal crust.

▼ Moss and Algae
(continued)

Appearance

- Moss: Low-growing plants that form a mat and have a velvety appearance and feel (photos 3.15 and 3.16)
- Algae: Greenish to brown, slimy scum that eventually turns to a greenish black crust on the soil surface (photo 3.17)

Problem Description

- These are indicator plants for areas of dense shade; low **pH**; compacted, wet soils; poor air circulation; and poor drainage but can also occur in well-fertilized, sunny locations
- Moss and algae are competitive when environmental conditions are unfavorable for **turf** growth

Cultural Options

- Rake out moss and algae and reseed areas
- Selectively remove or prune trees to enhance air movement and light penetration
- Reduce **compaction** and improve drainage
- Maintain adequate fertility
- Plant shade-tolerant species

University of Nebraska

Photo 3.18   Nitrogen (N) deficiency.
Yellowing turf (arrow) is a sign of N deficiency.

Rossi

Photo 3.19   Phosphorus (P) deficiency.
Dark areas (arrows) are a sign of P deficiency.

▼ Nutrient Deficiencies
(continued)

Appearance

- Nitrogen (N) deficiencies appear yellow with reduced **turf** density (photo 3.18)
- Phosphorus (P) deficiencies appear as a dark green to purplish color on older leaves, especially in seedings (photo 3.19)
- Potassium (K) deficiencies appear as yellowing and marginal browning of older leaves

Problem Description

- Soil tests are critical to determine nutrient deficiencies
- Soil **pH** should ideally be maintained in the 6–7 pH range to maximize nutrient use

Cultural Options

- Soil nutrition should be based on soil test results and species' requirements

▼ Pesticide and Chemical Injury

Photo 3.20   Pesticide and chemical injury.

Appearance
- Symptoms are variable and may include **chlorosis**, leaf speckling, curling, scorching, or death

Problem Description
- Damage will usually appear in the pattern in which the material was applied, leaked, or spilled (photo 3.20)

Cultural Options
- Thoroughly wash the area
- Consider using activated charcoal to absorb the chemical if it was recently applied

▼ Scalding/Flood Damage

Photo 3.21   Scalding/flood damage.
Note low wet area (arrow).

Appearance
- Dead brown areas appear a few days after water recedes (photo 3.21)

Problem Description
- Plant suffocates from lack of oxygen
- Severe on plants in standing water on hot, sunny days

Cultural Options
- Improve drainage
- Alleviate **compaction**
- Squeegee wet areas during periods of high temperatures

▼ Scalping

Photo 3.22   Scalping.
High spot in lawn scalped by mower.

Appearance

- Yellow to brown **turf** plants cut significantly shorter than the maintained height of cut (photo 3.22)

Problem Description

- A result of uneven surfaces, excessive **thatch**, close mowing, or rapid reduction in height of cut

- **Bunch grasses** (such as **perennial** ryegrass and fescues) may require reseeding; **stoloniferous** grasses (such as creeping bentgrass) and **rhizomatous** grasses (such as Kentucky bluegrass) usually recover

Cultural Options

- Maintain thatch at less than 0.5 inch
- Never remove more than one-third of the leaf **blade** at each mowing

▼ Shade

Photo 3.23   Shade.
Thin turf from low light (arrow).

Photo 3.24   Moss in low light.

Shade continued on page 40 ▶

▼ Shade
(continued)

Appearance

- Reduced turfgrass vigor (photo 3.23, page 39)
- Thin, spindly, pale green leaves; grass plants have shallow roots
- Thin **stand** with an increase in weed and moss problems (photo 3.24, page 39)

Problem Description

- Limited light for the grass reduces **photosynthesis** in the plant
- Grass and tree roots are competing for nutrients

Cultural Options

- Consider alternative groundcovers such as mulch
- Consider using fine fescues, which are the most shade-tolerant of all **cool-season turfgrasses** (although most grasses will not survive in dense shade)
- Selectively prune trees to improve light infiltration so plants receive four to six hours of direct sunlight

▼ Shallow Soil

Photo 3.25   Shallow soil, cross-section.
Note layering and shallow depth of topsoil (bracket).

Appearance

- **Turf** has patches or streaks of wilt
- Turf is invaded by both **annual** grasses (such as crabgrass) and broadleaf weeds

Problem Description

- Problem will appear in areas of construction dumping, septic areas, and rock outcroppings
- Turf in shallow soil will show drought stress sooner than turf in deeper soils

Cultural Options

- Concrete, bricks, lumber, rocks, and other debris should be removed to alleviate the problem
- Import 2–4 inches of topsoil; **cultivate** original soil to prevent layering (photo 3.25)
- Increase soil organic matter by **topdressing** with **compost** or other high-organic-matter material, **aerate**, and rake evenly

▼ Thatch

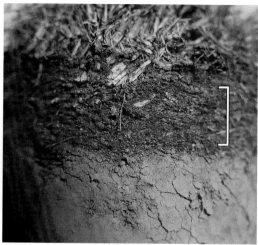

Photo 3.26   Thatch.
Note organic matter accumulation (bracket).

Appearance

- Layer of dead, decomposing plant matter between the **turf** plants and the soil (photo 3.26)

Problem Description

- Small amounts of **thatch** (less than 0.5 inch) insulate the soil, cushion the surface, and support an active microbial population

▼ Thatch

- A thick layer of thatch (more than 1 inch) will become water-repellent (**hydrophobic**) and reduce air and water movement as well as fertilizer and pesticide effectiveness

- Roots, **stolons**, and **rhizomes** will grow into excessive thatch layers; as a result, plants will be less tolerant of heat, drought, insect, and disease problems

- Excessive thatch accumulation has been associated with **acidic** soil conditions

Cultural Options

- **Core cultivate**, let plugs dry, break up plugs, and return plug material to the surface to serve as **topdressing**

- Maintain an adequate topdressing program to match turf growth

- If acidic soil conditions exist, apply lime

▼ Winter Desiccation

Photo 3.27   Winter desiccation.
Note bleached-out blades of turfgrass.

Appearance
- Irregular patches or streaks in the **turf**
- **Blades** of turfgrass appear bleached out (photo 3.27)

Problem Description
- Plants easily separate from the soil surface
- Occurs as a result of drying winds on elevated, exposed areas of frozen ground that lack snow cover

Cultural Options
- Heavy **topdressing** (not brushed in) and winter blankets can be used on putting greens
- Lightly water when temperatures go above 50°F (10°C)

CHAPTER FOUR

Diseases

The disease chapter is divided into three sections by season: late fall to early spring, spring and fall, and summer. See pages 4–5 for a timeline that shows what time of year certain diseases are likely to occur.

The discussion for each disease in this chapter is divided into six sections. The Causal Agent section lists the pathogen that causes the disease. The Appearance from a Distance and Appearance Close-Up sections describe how the disease will be noticeable to the turfgrass manager. The Ideal Conditions and Species Affected sections describe under which environmental conditions and on which turfgrass species the disease usually occurs. Finally, the Cultural Options section lists possible methods for managing the disease and ways to avoid reinfection.

A table of contents for this chapter is included on the following page. Terms defined in the glossary are in **bold** throughout the chapter.

Contents: Diseases

Late Fall to Early Spring

▼ Pink Snow Mold

Photo 4.1 Pink snow mold damage (from a distance).

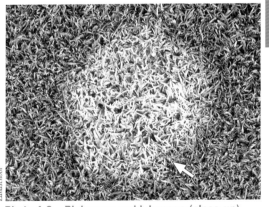

Photo 4.2 Pink snow mold damage (close-up).
Note pink margin (arrow).

Pink Snow Mold continued on page 48 ▶

Causal Agent

- *Microdochium nivale*

Appearance from a Distance

- Orange-brown to bleached to light gray, circular patches 2–10 inches in diameter (photo 4.1, page 47)

- Fluffy white to salmon pink mixture of fungal strands (**mycelia**) and **spores** visible at the edge of the patch

Appearance Close-Up

- Wet **turf**: Water-soaked spots with a pink outer margin (photo 4.2, page 47)

- Dry turf: Bleached spots and matted turf

- No brown to black fungal structures (**sclerotia**) as found in gray snow mold or *Typhula* blight (see page 50)

Ideal Conditions

- Cool (32°–50°F/0°–10°C), wet weather

- Severe damage under heavy, wet snow on unfrozen ground from late fall to late spring

▼ Pink Snow Mold
(continued)

Species Affected
- All **cool-season turfgrasses**, especially **perennial** ryegrass

Cultural Options
- Apply moderate nitrogen (N) levels during late summer and fall; avoid excessive late-season growth

- Prevent snow compaction; use snow fences to prevent drifting snow; physically remove snow

- Maintain a low soil **pH** (5.7–6.3) and balanced soil fertility

- Mow at recommended height until grass is **dormant** to prevent excessive top growth and **lodging**

- Use resistant varieties

▼ *Typhula* Blight / Gray Snow Mold

Photo 4.3 Gray snow mold (from a distance).

Photo 4.4 Gray snow mold (close-up).
Damage from gray snow mold under snow (arrow).

▼ *Typhula* Blight / Gray Snow Mold
(continued)

Causal Agent
- *Typhula incarnata* and *T. ishikariensis*

Appearance from a Distance
- Circular patches of dead, bleached to tan-colored areas up to several feet in diameter (photo 4.3)

Appearance Close-Up
- Water-soaked, matted **turf** covered with white to gray-white fungal threads (photo 4.4)
- Tiny (0.2- to 5.0-millimeter), round, reddish brown to black fungal structures called **sclerotia** on infected leaves
- Dry leaves are gray to silvery white with no fungal threads evident, brittle, and crusty over the patch

Ideal Conditions
- Cold temperatures (32°–45°F/0°–7°C) and prolonged snow cover
- Snow cover over wet, unfrozen ground
- Usually follows snow melt in late winter
- High levels of **soluble** nitrogen (N) applied before shoot growth ceases in late fall can increase likelihood of disease

Typhula Blight/Gray Snow Mold continued on page 52 ▶

▼ *Typhula* Blight / Gray Snow Mold
(continued)

Ideal Conditions *(continued)*
- Heavy straw mulches, a covering of tree leaves, or a tall turf canopy can increase likelihood of disease

Species Affected
- All **cool-season turfgrasses**, especially **perennial** ryegrass

Cultural Options
- Avoid applications of N after October 1 until the top growth ceases
- Improve drainage
- Prevent compaction of snow and use snow fences or barriers to prevent drifts
- Melt snow with darkening agents such as **organic fertilizer** or **compost**
- In spring, rake affected turf, remove debris, lightly fertilize, and reseed with a soil/seed patch mixture
- Mow at recommended height until grass is **dormant** to prevent excessive top growth and **lodging**

▼ Basal Rot Anthracnose

Photo 4.5 **Basal rot anthracnose (from a distance).** Note yellowish flecked areas.

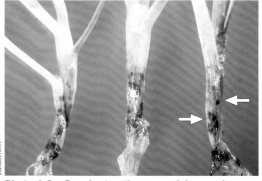

Photo 4.6 **Basal rot anthracnose (close-up).** Note acervuli — black fungal structures (arrows).

Basal Rot Anthracnose continued on page 54 ▶

▼ Basal Rot Anthracnose
(continued)

Causal Agent
- *Colletotrichum graminicola*

Appearance from a Distance
- Small, irregular patches (1–20 inches across) of reddish brown to tan **turf** (photo 4.5, page 53)

Appearance Close-Up
- Stem **lesions** appear water-soaked, then turn dark
- Central shoot of the infected plants turns yellow or orangish red
- Shoot base detaches easily and is blackened
- Grayish brown to black fungal structures (**acervuli**) may cover stem bases (photo 4.6, page 53)

Ideal Conditions
- Cool to warm (55°–70°F/13°–21°C), wet weather
- Stressed turf more prone to attack
- Leaf wetness required for infection

Species Affected
- Bentgrass and annual bluegrass
- Primarily a problem on golf courses

Cultural Options
- Reduce **compaction**
- Limit **thatch** to less than 0.75 inch
- Reduce leaf wetness
- Water to avoid drought stress

▼ Cool-Season *Pythium* Root and Crown Rot

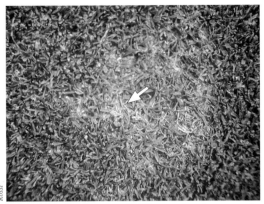

Rossi

Photo 4.7   Cool-season *Pythium* root and crown rot.
Note thin turf (arrow).

Causal Agent

- *Pythium* species

Appearance from a Distance

- Circular patches ranging from 1 to 6 inches in diameter or diffuse, **chlorotic** areas of **turf** (photo 4.7)

Appearance Close-Up

- **Crowns** may appear water-soaked
- Roots are stunted, thin, grayish white to brown

Cool-Season *Pythium* Root and Crown Rot
continued on page 56 ▶

▼ Cool-Season *Pythium* Root and Crown Rot
(continued)

Ideal Conditions
- Cool (32°–60°F/0°–16°C), wet conditions
- Spreads in free water and is enhanced by poor drainage
- More likely in low-light, high-traffic, closely mown areas

Species Affected
- Primarily annual bluegrass and bentgrass greens, but all **cool-season turfgrasses** may be affected
- Primarily a problem on golf courses

Cultural Options
- Avoid excessive springtime applications of nitrogen (N)
- Improve drainage, increase light, and raise mowing height
- Consider **composts** that can reduce disease severity

▼ Dollar Spot

Photo 4.8 Dollar spot (from a distance).

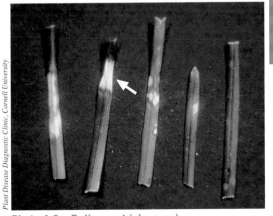

Photo 4.9 Dollar spot (close-up).
Note hourglass lesions (arrow).

Dollar Spot continued on page 58 ▶

Diseases   57

▼ Dollar Spot
(continued)

Causal Agent
- *Sclerotinia homoeocarpa*

Appearance from a Distance
- On closely mown **turf**: Collection of silver-dollar-size, tannish brown to whitish spots; turf appears speckled or mottled (photo 4.8, page 57)
- On residential turf: Collection of 1- to 6-inch-diameter bleached white patches

Appearance Close-Up
- Hourglass **lesions** on leaves are bleached in the center with tan to red-brown margins (photo 4.9, page 57)

Ideal Conditions
- Warm days (60°–90°F/16°–32°C) and cool nights (above 50°F/10°C)
- Prolonged leaf wetness, **dew**, and high **humidity**
- Dry soils with low nitrogen (N) fertility

Species Affected
- All **cool-season turfgrasses**

Cultural Options
- Maintain adequate fertility
- Reduce **compaction** and limit **thatch** to less than 0.75 inch
- Minimize leaf wetness
- Water to avoid drought stress
- Plant tolerant **cultivars**

▼ Fairy Rings

Photo 4.10   Fairy rings.
Note dark rings (arrows).

Causal Agent
- Many species of **fungi** known as **basidiomycetes**

Appearance from a Distance
- Large circles or arches, 1–30 feet in diameter and with an outer band of dark green, lush **turf** (photo 4.10)
- May have mushrooms in the outer band of turf, which is generally 4–8 inches wide

Appearance Close-Up
- White fungal strands (**mycelia**) in the soil and **thatch** behind the actively growing ring

Fairy Rings continued on page 60 ▶

▼ Fairy Rings
(continued)

Ideal Conditions
- Cool temperatures (45°–60°F/7°–16°C) and adequate soil moisture favor activity

Species Affected
- All **cool-season turfgrasses**

Cultural Options
- Irrigate to prevent drought stress

- Aerify soil

- Remove infested soil (20 inches in front and back of the ring to a depth of 8–30 inches) and **renovate**

- Fertilize to mask symptom expression

▼ Necrotic Ring Spot

Photo 4.11   Necrotic ring spot (from a distance).

Photo 4.12   Necrotic ring spot (close-up).
Note frog-eye patch (arrow).

Causal Agent

• *Leptosphaeria korrae*

Necrotic Ring Spot continued on page 62 ▶

▼ Necrotic Ring Spot
(continued)

Appearance from a Distance
- Light green to yellow patches 3–24 inches across or rings with green, healthy **turf** or weeds recolonizing infection centers (frog-eye patches) (photos 4.11 and 4.12, page 61)

Appearance Close-Up
- Light tan and matted patches
- Blackened roots and **rhizomes**
- Plants are easily removed from the soil

Ideal Conditions
- Cool to warm (50°–75°F/10°–24°C), wet weather
- Disease most common on two- to four-year-old turf
- Stress, **compaction**, drought, and high temperatures (above 80°F/27°C) enhance symptom expression
- Excessive nitrogen (N) applications (more than 0.5 pound per 1,000 square feet per application) increase severity

Species Affected
- Bentgrass, bluegrass, and fine fescue

Cultural Options
- Avoid excessive applications of water-**soluble** N; use natural organic N sources
- Irrigate to reduce stress
- Increase mowing height
- Reduce compaction and **thatch** (less than 0.5 inch)
- Use tolerant **cultivars**

▼ Pink Patch

Landschoot

Photo 4.13   Pink patch.
Note pink, gelatinous structure (arrow).

Causal Agent
- *Limonomyces roseipellis*

Appearance from a Distance
- Straw-colored, circular patches (4–20 inches across) or **blighted** areas

Appearance Close-Up
- Pink, gelatinous fungal tufts (**mycelia**) starting at leaf margins (photo 4.13)
- No "red threads" as found in red thread (see page 67)

Pink Patch continued on page 64 ▶

▼ Pink Patch
(continued)

Ideal Conditions
- Cool (50°–75°F/10°–24°C), wet weather favors activity
- Often found on the same plant as red thread (see page 67)

Species Affected
- **Perennial** ryegrass, fine fescues, Kentucky bluegrass, and bentgrasses

Cultural Options
- Maintain adequate and balanced fertility
- Reduce leaf wetness
- Selectively prune vegetation to increase air circulation
- Moderately resistant **cultivars** are available

▼ Powdery Mildew

Photo 4.14   Powdery mildew.
Note powdery film (arrow).

Causal Agent

- *Erysiphe graminis*

Appearance from a Distance

- Large, irregular patches of **turf** appear to have been dusted with white powder

Appearance Close-Up

- White to light gray, powdery fungal strands (**mycelia**) and **spores** on the leaf surface (photo 4.14)

- Infected leaves turn yellow, then tan, then brown

Powdery Mildew continued on page 66 ▶

▼ Powdery Mildew
(continued)

Ideal Conditions

- Cool (55°–72°F/13°–22°C), cloudy, humid weather
- Disease is more severe in shaded areas and areas with poor air circulation

Species Affected

- Kentucky bluegrass and fine fescue

Cultural Options

- Improve light penetration and air circulation by selectively pruning trees, shrubs, or brush
- Use shade-tolerant **cultivars**
- Water as needed to avoid drought stress
- Maintain adequate fertility but avoid excessive growth

▼ Red Thread

Photo 4.15   Red thread (from a distance).

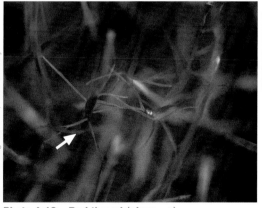

Photo 4.16   Red thread (close-up).
Note red thread (arrow).

Red Thread continued on page 68 ▶

▼ Red Thread
(continued)

Causal Agent
- *Laetisaria fuciformis*

Appearance from a Distance
- Circular or irregular patches, red to tan in color and 1.5–20 inches in diameter (photo 4.15, page 67)

Appearance Close-Up
- Infected leaves have a scorched or ragged appearance
- Death is from the tip of the leaf downwards
- On cool, wet days, "red threads" protrude from leaf tips (photo 4.16, page 67)
- Pink, gelatinous fungal strands (**mycelia**) that look and feel slimy
- **Fungus** is aggressive and can **blight** the leaf within two days of infection

Ideal Conditions
- Cool (40°–70°F/4°–21°C), wet conditions
- Often found along with pink patch (see page 63)
- Wind, running water, people, equipment, and animals spread the **pathogen**

Species Affected
- **Perennial** ryegrass and fine fescue are most susceptible; may also occur on bentgrass, tall fescue, and bluegrasses

Cultural Options
- Same as those for pink patch (see page 63)

▼ Spring/Fall Leaf Blight

Photo 4.17   Spring/fall leaf blight (from a distance).

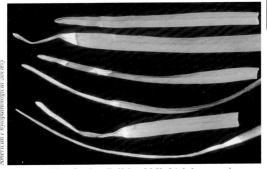

Photo 4.18   Spring/fall leaf blight (close-up).
Leaves die back from the tip and are tan or bleached in appearance.

Spring/Fall Leaf Blight continued on page 70 ▶

▼ Spring/Fall Leaf Blight
(continued)

Photo 4.19   Spring/fall leaf blight (close-up).
Tiny brown and black fungal structures dot the leaf tissue.

Causal Agents
- *Ascochyta* and *Leptosphaerulina* species

Appearance from a Distance
- Large areas of **turf** become **blighted** or patchy (photo 4.17, page 69)

Appearance Close-Up
- Individual leaves die back from the tip and are tan or bleached in appearance (photo 4.18, page 69)
- **Lesions** are possible
- Tiny brown and black fungal structures dot the dead leaf tissue (photo 4.19)

▼ Spring/Fall Leaf Blight
(continued)

Ideal Conditions

- Warm (60°–80°F/16°–27°C), humid conditions

- Disease is more severe on stressed turf, newly sodded areas, and turf that has been treated with grass **herbicide**

Species Affected

- All **cool-season turfgrasses**

Cultural Options

- Maintain adequate fertility

- Mow at species' recommended height when turf is dry

- Minimize leaf wetness

- Avoid herbicide applications or sodding when long periods of hot, humid weather are expected

▼ Spring/Fall Leaf Spots and Melting Out

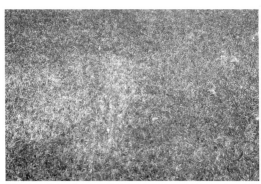

Photo 4.20 Spring/fall leaf spots and melting out (from a distance).

Photo 4.21 Spring/fall leaf spots and melting out (close-up).

▼ Spring/Fall Leaf Spots and Melting Out
(continued)

Causal Agents

- *Drechslera*, *Bipolaris*, and *Curvularia* species

Appearance from a Distance

- **Turf** appears yellow and thin (photo 4.20)

- Irregular patches of tan to reddish brown turf; resembles dull mower injury (see page 26)

Appearance Close-Up

- Leaves have oblong dark spots with tan centers that are surrounded by a yellow, brown, or reddish brown margin

- **Lesions** appear as spots or blotches near the leaf tip and vary in color from grayish green to purple

- Dieback is from the tip downwards

- Tiny, round, brown to black fungal structures appear in the dead areas of older lesions (photo 4.21)

Spring/Fall Leaf Spots and Melting Out
continued on page 74 ▶

▼ Spring/Fall Leaf Spots and Melting Out
(continued)

Ideal Conditions

- Cool to warm (40°–80°F/4°–27°C), moist, wet weather

- Wind, equipment, animals, and people easily spread diseases

Species Affected

- Kentucky bluegrasses, **perennial** ryegrasses, and fescues

Cultural Options

- Use resistant **cultivars** of tall fescue and Kentucky bluegrass

- Maintain moderate fertility but avoid excessive growth

- Mow at recommended height when turf is dry; low cut height can enhance symptom expression

- Water to avoid drought stress

- Minimize leaf wetness

- Limit **thatch** to 0.75 inch

▼ Yellow Patch

Landschoot

Photo 4.22   Yellow patch.
Note yellow ring (arrow).

Causal Agent

- *Rhizoctonia cerealis*

Appearance from a Distance

- Yellow to straw-colored patches or rings up to
  several feet in diameter that may have a bull's-
  eye or "target" appearance due to the healthy,
  unaffected **turf** in the center of the patches
  (photo 4.22)

Appearance Close-Up

- Individual plants may have tan **lesions** with
  dark brown margins

Yellow Patch continued on page 76 ▶

▼ Yellow Patch
(continued)

Ideal Conditions
- Cool (below 60°F/16°C), wet conditions
- High nitrogen (N) fertility can increase severity

Species Affected
- Bluegrass, bentgrass, and tall fescue

Cultural Options
- Use balanced N, phosphorus (P), and potassium (K) fertility
- Reduce leaf wetness
- Reduce **thatch** to less than 0.75 inch
- Avoid late fall fertilization prior to **dormancy**
- Usually, damage is not permanent

▼ Yellow Tuft (Downy Mildew)

Photo 4.23
Yellow tuft
(from a
distance).
Note yellow
flecking.

Photo 4.24   Yellow tuft (close-up).
Note excessive tillering (arrow).

Causal Agent

• *Sclerophthora macrophoma*

Yellow Tuft (Downy Mildew) continued on page 78 ▶

▼ Yellow Tuft/Downy Mildew
(continued)

Appearance from a Distance
- Yellow, speckled appearance with patches 0.5–4 inches in diameter (photo 4.23, page 77)

Appearance Close-Up
- Dense clusters of easily removed **tillers** that appear as tufts or **witches' broom** (photo 4.24, page 77)
- Yellow leaves and short roots

Ideal Conditions
- Cool (40°–70°F/4°–21°C), wet weather
- **Pathogen** needs free water (poor drainage, overirrigation) to spread
- New plantings are most susceptible, and high nitrogen (N) levels can increase severity

Species Affected
- Bentgrasses, fine fescues, **perennial** ryegrasses, and Kentucky bluegrass

Cultural Options
- Maintain active but not lush growth; avoid excessive N
- Mask symptoms by applying 1 ounce of iron sulfate per 1,000 square feet every two to four weeks
- Improve drainage
- Reduce leaf wetness and avoid overwatering
- Reduce or alleviate **compaction**

▼ Brown Patch

American Phytopathological Society

Photo 4.25   Brown patch (from a distance).

Rossi

Photo 4.26   Smoke ring associated with brown patch.

Brown Patch continued on page 80 ▶

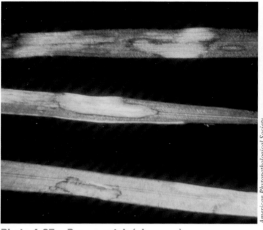

American Phytopathological Society

Photo 4.27   Brown patch (close-up).

Causal Agent

- *Rhizoctonia solani*

Appearance from a Distance

- On closely mown **turf**: Circular or irregular patches a few inches to several feet across that fade to light brown (photo 4.25, page 79)
- On closely mown turf: Smoke rings may be visible in early morning hours during hot, humid weather (photo 4.26, page 79)
- On higher cut turf: Large, diffuse areas of **blighted** turf; no distinct patch margins

▼ Brown Patch
(continued)

Appearance Close-Up
- Tan **lesions** with a dark brown margin (photo 4.27)

Ideal Conditions
- Warm temperatures (above 65°F/18°C) that persist into the evening (remaining above 60°F/16°C)
- Rainy, humid weather with prolonged leaf wetness
- Increased severity with excessive nitrogen (N) and low phosphorus (P) and potassium (K) levels

Species Affected
- All **cool-season turfgrasses**

Cultural Options
- Maintain moderate, balanced fertility
- Minimize leaf wetness
- Alleviate **compaction** and maintain **thatch** less than 0.75 inch
- Promote good surface drainage
- Selectively prune trees and shrubs to increase air circulation
- Use tolerant **cultivars**

▼ Dollar Spot

See page 57.

▼ Foliar Anthracnose

Plant Disease Diagnostic Clinic, Cornell University

Photo 4.28   Foliar anthracnose (from a distance).

Plant Disease Diagnostic Clinic, Cornell University

Photo 4.29   Foliar anthracnose (close-up).
Note acervuli — black fungal structures (arrow).

▼ Foliar Anthracnose
(continued)

Causal Agent
- *Colletotrichum graminicola*

Appearance from a Distance
- Yellow to brown, irregularly shaped patches from a few inches to several feet across (photo 4.28)

Appearance Close-Up
- Reddish brown then yellow **lesions** sometimes present on the leaves and leaf **sheaths**
- Tiny, black, hairlike fungal structures (**acervuli**) often present on lower leaves or plant parts (photo 4.29)

Ideal Conditions
- Warm (above 78°F/26°C), wet, humid weather
- Severe on plants in compacted, infertile, dry soil and in areas with excessive **thatch**

Species Affected
- Primarily annual bluegrass and bentgrasses

Cultural Options
- Maintain adequate fertility
- Alleviate **compaction** and limit thatch to less than 0.75 inch
- Minimize leaf wetness
- Irrigate to prevent drought stress

▼ Gray Leaf Spot

Photo 4.30   Gray leaf spot (from a distance).
Higher cut turf is injured first (arrow).

Causal Agent
- *Pyricularia grisea*

Appearance from a Distance
- Severely affected **turf** appears heat- or drought-stressed
- Higher cut turf is injured first (photo 4.30)

Appearance Close-Up
- Small brown spots expand rapidly into round to oblong **lesions** that have a tan to blue-gray center and irregular purple to brown margins that may or may not have a **chlorotic** halo surrounding the outside of the lesion

▼ Gray Leaf Spot
(continued)

- **Blighting** can kill plants in 48 hours
- During **spore** production, the blighted leaves can have a gray-white felt appearance

Ideal Conditions
- Warm temperatures (above 75°F/24°C) with high **humidity** and prolonged hours of leaf wetness
- On golf courses, the **pathogen** attacks the roughs and fairways
- Increased severity on newly seeded turf

Species Affected
- Ryegrasses and tall fescues

Cultural Options
- Avoid quick-release or high-nitrogen (N) applications during hot, wet, humid conditions
- Minimize leaf wetness
- Irrigate to avoid drought stress
- Improve drainage
- Alleviate **compaction**

▼ Necrotic Ring Spot

See page 61.

▼ *Pythium* Blight

Photo 4.31 *Pythium* blight (from a distance).
Damage follows drainage pattern (arrows).

Photo 4.32 *Pythium* blight (close-up).
Mycelia present in early morning hours.

▼ *Pythium* Blight
(continued)

Causal Agent
- *Pythium* species

Appearance from a Distance
- Circular, bluish to reddish brown patches 1–6 inches across that appear quickly and enlarge rapidly (photo 4.31)

Appearance Close-Up
- Water-soaked, slimy leaves
- Fluffy, grayish white, cottony fungal threads (**mycelia**) present in the early morning hours (photo 4.32)
- Infected leaves become tan to brown, shrivel, and mat when dry

Ideal Conditions
- High temperatures (above 90˚F/32˚C) and **humidity** that persist into the evening (remaining above 70˚F/21˚C) and a **relative humidity** above 90%
- Prolonged leaf wetness
- Poor drainage and **thatchy turf**
- Spreads by free water (may follow a drainage pattern; see photo 4.31), **clippings**, equipment, and shoes

Pythium Blight continued on page 88 ▶

▼ *Pythium* Blight
(continued)

Ideal Conditions *(continued)*
- Excessive nitrogen (N) fertility and calcium (Ca) deficiency can increase severity and incidence

Species Affected
- Primarily seedlings or immature **stands** of **perennial** ryegrass, annual bluegrass, and bentgrasses

Cultural Options
- Maintain moderate N and optimum Ca levels (as per soil test recommendations)
- Improve drainage
- Minimize leaf wetness and watering late in the day
- Avoid mowing and trafficking susceptible turf when fungal threads are present
- Use fungicide-treated seed when planting in hot, humid weather

▼ Rusts

Plant Disease Diagnostic Clinic, Cornell University

Photo 4.33   Rusts (close-up).
Note orange pustules on leaf blade.

Causal Agent
- *Puccinia* species

Appearance from a Distance
- Thin, weakened **turf** that appears covered with an orange-red dust

Appearance Close-Up
- Yellow, orange, red, or brown powdery **pustules** that elongate parallel to the leaf vein and on stems (photo 4.33)
- Powder will discolor shoes and clothing

Rusts continued on page 90 ▶

▼ Rusts
(continued)

Ideal Conditions
- Warm nights (68°–86°F/20°–30°C), wet leaves, and low light intensity (shady sites or cloudy weather)
- Most severe mid to late summer into fall when turf is not actively growing or under stress

Species Affected
- All **cool-season turfgrasses**, especially **perennial** ryegrass

Cultural Options
- Maintain fertility for active growth throughout the season
- Minimize leaf wetness
- Irrigate to prevent drought stress
- Use tolerant **cultivars**

▼ Stripe Smut

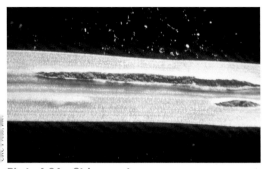

Photo 4.34   Stripe smut.
Note parallel orientation.

Causal Agent
- *Ustilago striiformis*

Appearance from a Distance
- Irregular, yellowing, stunted patches

Appearance Close-Up
- Infected leaves have parallel yellow streaks that may change to gray black (photo 4.34)
- Leaves turn brown, wither, shred between veins, and curl from the tip downwards

Stripe Smut continued on page 92 ▶

▼ Stripe Smut
(continued)

Ideal Conditions

- Infection occurs during cool (50°–65°F/10°–18°C), wet conditions; disease favors excessive leaf wetness and low to moderate soil moisture

- Disease is severe in long, hot, dry periods on **turf** older than four years

Species Affected

- Kentucky bluegrass, bentgrass, and occasionally tall fescue and **perennial** ryegrass

Cultural Options

- Use moderate fertility levels to promote active but not excessive growth

- Irrigate to avoid drought stress

- Minimize leaf wetness

- Use tolerant **cultivars**

▼ Summer Leaf Spots

Photo 4.35   Summer leaf spot.

Causal Agents
- *Bipolaris* and *Curvularia* species

Appearance from a Distance
- Irregular patches or streaks of thin, ragged **turf**

Appearance Close-Up
- Yellowish to tan **lesions** with reddish brown margins and tip dieback (photo 4.35)

Ideal Conditions
- Warm (77°–95°F/25°–35°C), wet weather

Summer Leaf Spots continued on page 94 ▶

▼ Summer Leaf Spots
(continued)

Ideal Conditions *(continued)*
- Severe at high temperatures and in high-nitrogen (N) conditions

Species Affected
- All **cool-season turfgrasses**, primarily Kentucky bluegrass

Cultural Options
- Maintain moderate fertility

- Minimize leaf wetness

- Alleviate **compaction** and properly manage **thatch** (limit to 0.5–0.75 inch)

- Increase mowing height

▼ Summer Patch

Photo 4.36   Summer patch.

Causal Agent
- *Magnaporthe poae*

Appearance from a Distance
- Yellow to straw-colored circular patches (2–20 inches in diameter) that may coalesce (photo 4.36)
- Irregular patches, rings, and crescent patterns
- Slow-growing, thin, or wilted **turf**
- In a mix, bentgrass or weeds can colonize patch centers

Summer Patch continued on page 96 ▶

▼ Summer Patch
(continued)

Appearance Close-Up

- Grayish green to yellow to straw-colored leaves at high temperatures
- Lower plant parts darken and roots have brown-black fungal threads (**mycelia**) along the surface

Ideal Conditions

- Hot days (above 85°F/29°C) that persist into evening (remaining above 60°F/16°C) and rainy conditions
- Can be confused with heat stress, insect damage, or other diseases
- Infection occurs in late spring when soil temperatures exceed 65°F (18°C) at a 2-inch depth
- Symptoms appear in the summer (late June through late September)
- Spreads by dethatching, **cultivation** equipment, and infected sod
- Severe during hot, wet years on poorly drained, compacted sites
- Frequent watering, **pH** above 6.0, and low mowing height may increase severity

▼ Summer Patch
(continued)

Species Affected
- Bluegrass and fine fescue

Cultural Options
- Maintain adequate fertility with pH 5.5–6.0

- Improve drainage and irrigate to prevent drought stress

- Alleviate **compaction** and increase height of cut

- **Renovate** or overseed with **perennial** ryegrass, tall fescue, or tolerant **cultivars** of Kentucky bluegrass

▼ Take-All Patch

Photo 4.37   Take-all patch on bentgrass.
Note annual bluegrass regrowth in center of patch (arrow).

Causal Agent

- *Gaeumannomyces graminis* var. *avenae*

Appearance from a Distance

- Circular patches from 6 inches to 3 feet in diameter
- Weeds, annual bluegrass, or fine fescue can recolonize center of patch (photo 4.37)

Appearance Close-Up

- Lower plant parts become dark brown to black
- Dark strands of fungal threads appear parallel to the root surface
- Tiny black fungal structures (**perithecia**) visible in late spring or autumn on lower plant parts

▼ Take-All Patch
(continued)

Ideal Conditions

- Infection occurs in cool (50°–65°F/10°–18°C), wet weather
- Symptoms are most apparent in warm to hot temperatures (above 70°F/21°C) and dry weather
- Mechanical equipment, infected sod, or seed can spread disease
- Prevalent on moist, high-**pH**, and nutritionally unbalanced soils (liming enhances the disease)
- Soil conditions favoring disease are coarse texture, low organic content, recent fumigation, or high sand content

Species Affected

- Bentgrass
- Mostly a problem on golf courses

Cultural Options

- Apply acidifying fertilizers to lower soil pH to between 5.5 and 6.0 where possible (care should be taken to avoid applications at high temperatures to prevent fertilizer burn)
- Maintain balanced fertility
- Do not apply lime
- Improve drainage and alleviate **compaction**
- Avoid deep, frequent irrigation, especially with high-pH water

CHAPTER 5

Insects

Insects in this chapter are grouped into two categories: surface (found above soil level) and subsurface (found at or below soil level). See pages 6–7 for a **timeline** that shows what time of year certain insects are likely to be active.

The discussion for each insect is divided into four sections. The **Appearance of Damage** section describes the physical symptoms exhibited by turfgrass upon damage from the insect. The **Appearance of Insect** section describes the physical characteristics of both the immature and the mature insect; many times, damage is caused by an immature stage rather than the adult. The **Pest Information** section describes the insect's life cycle, the types of conditions under which the insect can usually be found, and any behavioral information that will help with identification. Finally, the **Damage Thresholds and Management** section gives damage **threshold** limits, sampling methods, control guidelines, and ways to strengthen turfgrass again the insect.

Terms defined in the glossary are in **bold** throughout the chapter (see **threshold** above).

Contents: Insects

NOTE: All given thresholds in this chapter are approximations only and must be viewed in light of the actual situation, including the value and condition of the **turf**, past history, likelihood of secondary damage by skunks (which appears as disturbed turf from skunks foraging for **grubs**), size of the infestation, control methods available, and so on.

Surface

▼ Annual Bluegrass Weevil
(Formerly *Hyperodes*)

Photo 5.1   Damage from annual bluegrass weevil.
Damage begins at edges (woodline) and moves inward (arrow).

Photo 5.2   Annual bluegrass weevil adult.
Note characteristic snout (arrow).

Rossi

Photo 5.3   Annual bluegrass weevil grub.
Note small size (arrow).

Appearance of Damage

- Infested **turf** turns yellow, wilts, and will not respond to watering (photo 5.1)
- Grass plants may break off in weakened stem areas

Appearance of Insect

- Adults are small, dark grayish brown to black beetles approximately 0.1 inch long with a broad, short snout (photo 5.2)

- Fifth **instar grubs** reach a maximum size of 0.2 inch long and are distinguished from other white grubs by the absence of legs (photo 5.3)

Annual Bluegrass Weevil continued on page 104 ▶

▼ Annual Bluegrass Weevil
(continued)

Pest Information
- Two generations per year
- Surface or **thatch** pest that burrows into the stems
- Adults overwinter in areas next to fairways, greens, and tees (especially where there is white pine litter) and crawl to nearby grassy areas between when forsythia is in full bloom and dogwood is in full bloom
- Damage begins at the edges of golf course fairways and greens and moves inward over the season (photo 5.1, page 102)
- Populations are often mixed with black turfgrass ataenius (see page 119)

Damage Thresholds and Management
- Use a **threshold** of 30 to 50 **larvae** per square foot
- Use a **cup cutter**, then flotation for sampling (see chapter 2, pages 13–14)
- Initiate control when adults are seen in the spring (when forsythia is in full bloom), and follow up with second generation adult control by monitoring for high populations in July
- Maintain sufficient soil moisture and proper fertility levels
- Consider debris removal in wooded areas to reduce overwintering habitat

▼ Bluegrass Billbug

NYSAES, Cornell University

Photo 5.4 Damage from bluegrass billbug.
Adult insects may be observed crawling over paved areas.

NYSAES, Cornell University

Photo 5.5 Bluegrass billbug adult.
Note snout (arrow).

Bluegrass Billbug continued on page 106 ▶

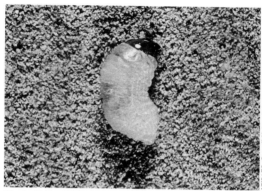

Photo 5.6 Bluegrass billbug grub.

Appearance of Damage

- Yellow to brown spots in the **turf** (photo 5.4, page 105) often resembling dollar spot (see page 57)

- Grass **crowns** are easily pulled from the soil, and a light brown, sawdustlike material can be observed in the root/crown area

Appearance of Insect

- Adult beetles are approximately 0.25 inch long and dark gray to black with an elongated snout (photo 5.5, page 105)

- Fifth **instar grubs** are up to 0.5 inch long and have no legs (photo 5.6)

▼ Bluegrass Billbug
(continued)

Pest Information
- One generation per year
- Beginning in mid May into June, adults may be observed crawling over paved areas, because a favorite overwintering site is the crevice between turf and pavement (photo 5.4, page 105)
- Surface or **thatch** pest that burrows into the stems
- Frequently occurs on higher cut turf and tends to be more of a problem on home lawns than on golf courses
- Adults chew an opening in the leaf **sheath** above the crown and deposit eggs
- Damage has been mistaken for drought, **dormancy**, or delayed greening up in the spring

Damage Thresholds and Management
- Anticipate damage to adjacent turf if one or more adults are observed per minute on pavement; this is the time for chemical control, if needed
- Maintain sufficient soil moisture and proper fertility levels
- Use **endophyte**-enhanced ryegrass and fescue that are resistant to or tolerant of billbug attack

▼ Hairy Chinch Bug

NYSAES, Cornell University

Photo 5.7   Damage from hairy chinch bug.

NYSAES, Cornell University

**Photo 5.8
Hairy chinch bug
adult.**
Adults are black.
Wings are shiny and
white with a black
spot.

Appearance of Damage

- Badly infested plants turn yellow then brown
  during the hot, dry months (photo 5.7)

▼ Hairy Chinch Bug
(continued)

Appearance of Insect
- Adults measure 0.1 inch long and are black with shiny white wings that have a black spot on them (photo 5.8)
- Older **nymphs** are less than 0.1 inch long and black with easily visible, developing wing pads

Pest Information
- One to two generations per year
- Surface or **thatch** pest that discolors leaves and stems
- Adults become active in temperatures above 45°F (7°C)
- Insects thrive in hot, dry weather in **turf** with heavy thatch
- Damage is often confused with drought injury or sunscald; however, turf does not respond to irrigation

Damage Thresholds and Management
- **Threshold** is 15 to 20 insects per square foot
- Begin to sample in spring when temperatures exceed 60°F (16°C) in areas that have a history of chinch bug damage
- Use flotation for sampling (see chapter 2, page 13)
- Maintain sufficient soil moisture and proper fertility levels
- Use **endophyte**-enhanced grass varieties that are tolerant of chinch bug damage
- Use resistant Kentucky bluegrass **cultivars**

▼ Sod Webworm Complex

Photo 5.9   Sod webworm complex adult.
Adult moth is whitish to a light gray or tan and has a snoutlike
projection from its head (arrow).

Photo 5.10   Sod webworm complex larvae.
Larvae have caterpillar-shaped bodies. In this photo, larvae are
feeding on a sheath.

Appearance of Damage

- Damage appears as dead spots 3–10 inches in
  diameter and tunnels constructed of silk with
  soil and grass **clippings** attached

▼ Sod Webworm Complex
(continued)

Appearance of Insect

- Adults may be seen facing downward on the turfgrass stem
- Adult moths are 0.5–0.75 inch long, whitish to a light gray or tan in color, and have a snoutlike projection from their heads (photo 5.9)
- **Larvae** have a caterpillar-shaped body, are 0.5–1 inch long, are gray to beige-brown with dark spots, and have three pair of front legs and five pair of back legs (photo 5.10)

Pest Information

- Two to three generations per year
- Webworms prefer a higher cut **turf** than cutworms
- Larvae can be expected two weeks after peak moth flights

Damage Thresholds and Management

- Generally, **threshold** is one to ten larvae per square yard
- Sample by using a disclosing solution, and insects will wriggle to the surface (see chapter 2, page 13)
- Maintain sufficient soil moisture and proper fertility levels

Subsurface

To sample subsurface insect populations for identification, use the soil examination method (see photos 5.11 and 5.12 below and figure 1.3, page 15). Cut three sides of a 1-square-foot **turf** area with a shovel. Peel back the sod layer to expose **grubs**, then examine grubs' **raster patterns** to identify the species (see "Raster Patterns of White Grubs" on the following page).

**Photo 5.11
Soil examination.**
To sample subsurface insect populations, peel back the turf layer to expose grubs and larvae.

**Photo 5.12
Soil examination (close-up).**
Examine the raster pattern on the grub to help identify the species. See figures 5.1–5.8 on pages 113–114 for raster patterns of white grubs.

Raster Patterns of White Grubs

Subsurface insects can often be identified by examining grubs found in the soil. It is important to know which species of white grub you are dealing with in order to implement the proper control strategies.

To identify the species, hold the grub between your thumb and forefinger so you can observe the tail end. A hand lens or magnifying lens will help. (Grubs range in size from about 0.75 to 2 inches long.) Each grub has an anal slit that may transverse the tail, or it may have a Y-shaped branch. In addition, there are spines or hairs in front of the slit that form a pattern (figures 5.1–5.8). Each species of white grub has its own distinct pattern of slit and spines (hairs).

Figure 5.1
Raster pattern of Asiatic garden beetle.
Branched anal slit with a semicircular row of spines in front of the anal slit.

Figure 5.3
Raster pattern of European chafer.
Y-shaped anal slit and two almost parallel rows of spines that diverge at the slit.

Figure 5.2
Raster pattern of black turfgrass ataenius.
Two distinct padlike structures on the abdomen on the tip of the anal slit.

Figure 5.4
Raster pattern of green June beetle.
Transverse anal slit with two short rows of spines just forward of the anal slit.

Continued on page 114 ▶

**Figure 5.5
Raster pattern of
Japanese beetle.**
Transverse anal slit with
a distinctive V-shaped
row of spines in front
of the anal slit.

**Figure 5.7
Raster pattern of
northern masked
chafer.**
Transverse anal slit with
no distinct pattern to the
spines.

**Figure 5.6
Raster pattern of June
beetle.**
V- or Y-shaped anal slit
with two rows of sharp
spines just forward of
the anal slit.

**Figure 5.8
Raster pattern of
oriental beetle.**
Transverse anal slit with
two parallel rows of spines
to the front of the slit.

▼ Asiatic Garden Beetle

Photo 5.13   Asiatic garden beetle adult.
Note raster pattern of grub (shown below).

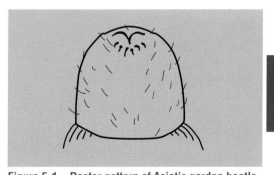

Figure 5.1   Raster pattern of Asiatic garden beetle.
Branched anal slit with a semicircular row of spines in front of
the anal slit. Third instar grubs can be up to 0.75 inch long.

Asiatic Garden Beetle continued on page 116 ▶

▼ Asiatic Garden Beetle
(continued)

Appearance of Damage
- Yellowing, wilting, thinning of **turf**; in severe cases, turf can be rolled back like a rug

Appearance of Insect
- Adults are up to 0.25 inch long and chestnut brown in color with yellow hairs on the underside (photo 5.13, page 115)
- Third **instar grubs** can be up to 0.75 inch long; are C-shaped and cream-colored with a brown head; and have a swollen, bulbous structure at the sides of the mouth
- **Raster pattern** is a transverse semicircular row of spines/hairs below a Y-shaped anal slit (figure 5.1, page 115)

Pest Information
- Subsurface pest that feeds at greater depths than Japanese or oriental beetles

Damage Thresholds and Management
- **Threshold** is 18 to 20 grubs per square foot
- Begin sampling in early August using a **cup cutter** (see chapter 2, page 14)
- Maintain sufficient soil moisture and proper fertility levels

▼ Black Cutworm

Photo 5.14   Black cutworm adult.
Adults are dull-colored moths.

Photo 5.15   Black cutworm larva.
Larvae appear as 1.2- to 1.75-inch-long caterpillars.

Black Cutworm continued on page 118 ▶

▼ Black Cutworm
(continued)

Appearance of Damage
- Damage appears as 1- to 2-inch dead spots that resemble ball marks on closely cut **turf**, with a pencil-sized hole in the middle

Appearance of Insect
- Adults are dull-colored moths with wing spans of 1.25–1.75 inches; wings are folded flat over the abdomen when at rest (photo 5.14, page 117)
- **Larvae** are 1.2- to 1.75-inch-long caterpillars and have three pair of legs at the front and five pair of legs at the back (photo 5.15, page 117)

Pest Information
- Two to three generations per year
- Cutworms will coil into a circle when disturbed
- **Perennial** pest of closely cut turf on golf courses

Damage Thresholds and Management
- **Threshold** is three to eight larvae per square yard
- Monitor the arrival of migrating moths from the South using **pheromone** traps; two weeks later, begin to sample greens
- Sample with disclosing solution; irritated worms will wriggle to the surface (see chapter 2, page 13)
- Maintain sufficient soil moisture and proper fertility levels so low pest levels can be tolerated without loss of turf
- Collect **clippings** and dispose of them at least 200 feet away from the putting green

▼ Black Turfgrass Ataenius

Photo 5.16   Damage from black turfgrass ataenius.

Photo 5.17   Black turfgrass ataenius.
Three stages: [Left] Grub — can be up to 1 inch long, arrow
shows location of raster pattern (see figure 5.2 on page 120);
[Middle] Pupa; [Right] Adult.

Black Turfgrass Ataenius continued on page 120 ▶

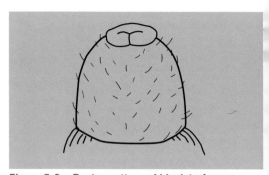

Figure 5.2   Raster pattern of black turfgrass ataenius.
Two distinct padlike structures on the abdomen on the tip of the anal slit. Grubs can be up to 1 inch long.

Appearance of Damage

- Yellowing, wilting, and thinning of **turf** (photo 5.16, page 119)

- In severe cases, turf can be rolled back like a rug

- Damage is often in large patches (up to 30 feet in diameter) that appear in June and August

Appearance of Insect

- Adults are shiny, black, and up to 0.2 inch long (similar in size to annual bluegrass weevil but without the snout) (photo 5.17, page 119)

- **Grubs** are C-shaped, up to 1 inch long, and cream-colored with a brown head and three pair of legs (photo 5.17, page 119)

- **Raster pattern** consists of two padlike structures on the tip of the abdomen above the anal slit (figure 5.2)

Pest Information

- One to two generations per year
- Smallest of the **scarab** turfgrass pests
- Third **instar** grub can be confused with first instar grubs like Japanese or oriental beetles, especially in August
- Subsurface pest attacks turfgrass roots
- Insect overwinters as an adult and in April to May migrates from woody areas to fairways, greens, and tees to mate and lay eggs
- Damage from the first generation appears in late May to June; damage from the second generation is evident in August through September
- Associated with high-organic-matter soils

Damage Thresholds and Management

- **Threshold** is 30 to 50 grubs per square foot
- Begin sampling in early to mid May for the first generation and in August to September for the second generation using a **cup cutter**, disclosing solution, or both (see chapter 2, pages 13–14)
- Maintain sufficient soil moisture and proper fertility levels

▼ European Chafer

Photo 5.18   European chafer adult.
Note raster pattern of grub (shown below).

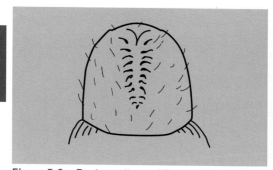

Figure 5.3   Raster pattern of European chafer.
Y-shaped anal slit and two almost parallel rows of spines that diverge at the slit. Grubs are slightly more than 1 inch long.

Appearance of Damage
- Yellowing, wilting, thinning of **turf**; in severe cases, the turf can be rolled back like a rug

Appearance of Insect
- Adults can be 0.5 inch long and a dull chestnut brown color (photo 5.18)
- Third **instar grubs** are typical C-shaped white grubs and slightly more than 1 inch long
- **Raster pattern** is two almost parallel rows of hairs that diverge below a Y-shaped anal slit (figure 5.3)

Pest Information
- One generation per year
- Can be a serious pest on home lawns and low-maintenance turf
- Feeds later into the fall and earlier in the spring than other grubs and can even resume feeding during warm spells in the winter

Damage Thresholds and Management
- **Threshold** is five to seven grubs per square foot
- Begin sampling in early August using a **cup cutter** (see chapter 2, page 14)
- Maintain sufficient soil moisture and proper fertility levels

▼ Green June Beetle

Photo 5.19   Green June beetle adult.

NYSAES, Cornell University

Photo 5.20   Green June beetle grub.
Grubs can be up to 2 inches long. Arrow shows location of
grub raster pattern (shown in figure 5.4).

NYSAES, Cornell University

▼ Green June Beetle
(continued)

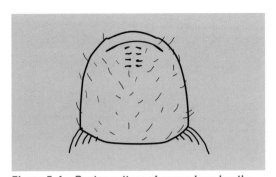

Figure 5.4   Raster pattern of green June beetle.
Transverse anal slit with two short rows of spines just forward of the anal slit. Grubs can be up to 2 inches long.

Appearance of Damage
- **Turf** wilts, and mounds and tunnels are visible
- Mounds resemble earthworm **castings**

Appearance of Insect
- Adults can be 1 inch long and are forest green with or without a tan stripe on each wing cover (photo 5.19)
- Third **instar grubs** can be 2 inches long and are broader than other white grubs (photo 5.20)
- **Raster pattern** consists of a transverse anal slit with two short rows of spines or hairs just forward of the anal slit (figure 5.4)

Green June Beetle continued on page 126 ▶

▼ Green June Beetle
(continued)

Pest Information
- When placed on any surface **ventral** side down, grubs will turn over and crawl on their backs
- One generation per year
- Damage to the turf is not from feeding but from constant burrowing and tunneling in the root zone

Damage Thresholds and Management
- At the present time, there are no damage **thresholds**
- Begin sampling in early August using a **cup cutter** (see chapter 2, page 14)
- Maintain sufficient soil moisture and proper fertility levels

▼ Japanese Beetle

NYSAES, Cornell University

Photo 5.21   Japanese beetle adult.

NYSAES, Cornell University

Photo 5.22   Japanese beetle grub.
Grubs can be up to 1 inch long. Arrow shows location of grub
raster pattern (shown in figure 5.5 on page 128).

Japanese Beetle continued on page 128 ▶

Figure 5.5   Raster pattern of Japanese beetle.
Transverse anal slit with a distinctive V-shaped row of spines in front of the anal slit. Grubs can be up to 1 inch long.

Appearance of Damage

- Yellowing, wilting, thinning of the **stand**; in severe cases, the **turf** can be rolled back like a rug

Appearance of Insect

- Adults are up to 0.5 inch with a bright, metallic green body and brown wing covers (photo 5.21, page 127)

- Third **instar grubs** can be 1 inch long, are C-shaped and cream-colored, and have a hindgut that is gray to black from accumulated fecal matter (photo 5.22, page 127)

- **Raster pattern** is a distinct "V" of spines/hairs below the transverse anal slit (figure 5.5)

▼ Japanese Beetle
(continued)

Pest Information

- One generation per year

- Subsurface pest attacks turfgrass roots

- Secondary damage to turf occurs from animals that feed on grubs, such as skunks, raccoons, and birds

- Adults are day flyers that defoliate many ornamental plants

Damage Thresholds and Management

- **Threshold** is eight to ten grubs per square foot

- Begin sampling in early to mid August using a **cup cutter** (see chapter 2, page 14)

- Adult populations can be monitored using traps baited with both a floral lure and sex **pheromones** (Note: Traps have never been shown to reduce grub damage.)

- Maintain sufficient soil moisture and proper fertility levels

▼ May or June Beetles

Photo 5.23   May or June beetle adult.

NYSAES, Cornell University

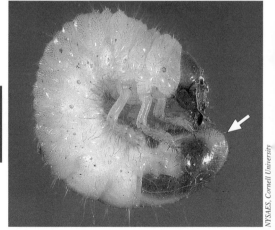

Photo 5.24   May or June beetle grub.
Grubs range in size from 1 to 1.5 inches long. Arrow shows location of grub raster pattern (shown in figure 5.6).

NYSAES, Cornell University

▼ May or June Beetles
(continued)

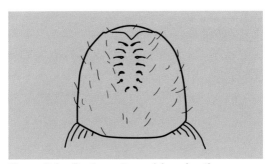

Figure 5.6   Raster pattern of June beetle.
V- or Y-shaped anal slit with two rows of sharp spines just
forward of the anal slit. Grubs range in size from 1 to 1.5
inches long.

Appearance of Damage
- Yellowing, wilting, and thinning of the **turf stand**

Appearance of Insect
- Adults can be 1 inch long and are various shades of brown, depending on the species (photo 5.23)
- Third **instar grubs** are C-shaped and range in size from 1 to 1.5 inches long when stretched out (photo 5.24)
- **Raster pattern** is a V- or Y-shaped anal slit with two rows of sharp spines just forward of the anal slit (figure 5.6)

May or June Beetles continued on page 132 ▶

▼ May or June Beetles
(continued)

Pest Information

- One generation every one to three years, depending on the species
- Large size of the grubs means fewer **larvae** can do more damage

Damage Thresholds and Management

- **Threshold** is three to four grubs per square foot
- Begin sampling in early to mid August using a **cup cutter** (see chapter 2, page 14)
- Maintain sufficient soil moisture and proper fertility levels so low pest levels can be tolerated without loss of turf

▼ Northern Masked Chafer

Photo 5.25   Northern masked chafer adult.

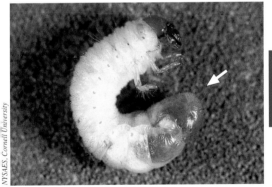

Photo 5.26   Northern masked chafer grub.
Grubs can be 1 inch long. Arrow shows location of grub raster
pattern (shown in figure 5.7, page 134).

Northern Masked Chafer continued on page 134 ▶

▼ Northern Masked Chafer
(continued)

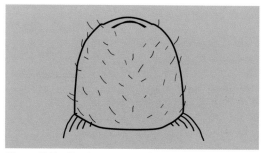

Figure 5.7   Raster pattern of northern masked chafer.
Transverse anal slit with no distinct pattern to the spines. Grubs can be 1 inch long.

Appearance of Damage
- Yellowing, wilting, thinning of **turf**; in serious cases, turf can be rolled back like a rug

Appearance of Insect
- Adult beetles are up to 0.5 inch long with yellow-brown bodies and chocolate brown heads (photo 5.25, page 133)
- Third **instar grubs** are C-shaped, can be 1 inch long, and are cream-colored with a chestnut brown head (photo 5.26, page 133)
- **Raster pattern** is 25 to 30 spines/hairs in no particular pattern below a transverse anal slit (figure 5.7)

▼ Northern Masked Chafer
(continued)

Pest Information
- One generation per year
- Subsurface pest attacks turfgrass roots

Damage Thresholds and Management
- **Threshold** is nine to ten grubs per square foot
- Begin sampling in early to mid August using a **cup cutter** (see chapter 2, page 14)
- Maintain sufficient soil moisture and proper fertility levels

▼ Oriental Beetle

NYSAES, Cornell University

Photo 5.27 Oriental beetle adult.

NYSAES, Cornell University

Photo 5.28 Oriental beetle grub.
Grubs can be 1 inch long when stretched out. Arrow shows
location of grub raster pattern (shown in figure 5.8).

▼ Oriental Beetle
(continued)

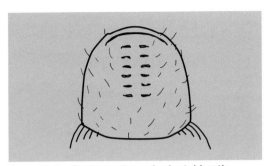

Figure 5.8   Raster pattern of oriental beetle.
Transverse anal slit with two parallel rows of spines to the front of the slit. Grubs can be 1 inch long when stretched out.

Appearance of Damage
- Yellowing, wilting, and thinning of the **stand**; in severe cases, **turf** can be rolled back like a rug

Appearance of Insect
- Adults are up to 0.5 inch long and vary in color from black or gray to straw with dark markings on the wing covers (photo 5.27)
- Third **instar grubs** are C-shaped, cream-colored, and can be 1 inch long when stretched out (photo 5.28)
- **Raster pattern** consists of two parallel rows of spines/hairs pointing to the median and a transverse anal slit (figure 5.8)

Oriental Beetle continued on page 138 ▶

▼ Oriental Beetle
(continued)

Pest Information

- One generation per year

- Subsurface pest attacks turfgrass roots

- Adult beetles are rarely seen and do little feeding damage compared to Japanese beetles

- Grubs can be very damaging to turf, because they may occur at levels of 40–50 per square foot

Damage Thresholds and Management

- **Threshold** is five to seven grubs per square foot

- Begin sampling with a **cup cutter** in early to mid August (see chapter 2, page 14)

- Maintain sufficient soil moisture and proper fertility levels so low pest levels can be tolerated without loss of turf

CHAPTER 6
Weeds

The key to weed management is to identify the factor that is causing the reduction in **turf** density. These factors could be related to mowing, fertilization, or irrigation practices.

The weeds in this chapter are divided into four groups: **perennials**, broadleaf; perennials, grasses or grasslike; **annuals**, winter; and annuals, summer. Weeds are arranged alphabetically within each group.

The discussion for each weed is divided into three sections. The **General Description** section describes the weed's physical characteristics, including growth habit, leaves, stems, flowers, and other reproductive structures. The **Reproduction** section describes how the weed is propagated. Finally, the **Location** section lists the types of areas in which the weed can usually be found.

A **timeline** showing the life cycles of weeds in this chapter can be found on pages 8–9. Terms defined in the glossary are in **bold** throughout the chapter (see **turf** and **perennials** above).

A table of contents for this chapter is included on the following page.

Contents: Weeds

Contents: Weeds

Perennial, Broadleaf

▼ Broadleaf Plantain
(Plantago major)

Photo 6.1   Broadleaf plantain.

General Description

- **Perennial**
- Closely related to blackseed plantain *(Plantago rugelii)*
- Large, **basal rosette** with broad, oval, wavy-edged leaves (photo 6.1)
- **Scapes** (long, erect, leafless flowering stalks) arise from the rosette
- Produces tiny, inconspicuous flowers for a short period from June to September

▼ Broadleaf Plantain
(continued)

Reproduction
- Seed germinates late spring through midsummer

Location
- Located in low- and high-maintenance **turf**, landscapes, nurseries, and orchards
- Prefers damp, nutrient-rich soils

▼ Buckhorn Plantain
(Plantago lanceolata)

Photo 6.2   Buckhorn plantain.
Note seed stalk (top arrow) and basal rosette (bottom arrow).

General Description

- **Perennial**
- Long, narrow, parallel-veined leaves forming a **basal rosette** (photo 6.2)
- Stems consist of long, leafless, ridged, unbranched stalks
- Brown, dense, conelike, cylindrical seedheads located at ends of stalks (photo 6.2)
- Flowers are tiny and individually indistinguishable and are produced on the seedhead in dense clusters
- Blooms in late May through September

▼ Buckhorn Plantain
(continued)

Reproduction
- Primarily produced by seed and new shoots at base of plant

Location
- In turfgrass, landscapes, orchards, roadsides, meadows, and waste places

▼ Common Blue Violet
(Viola papilionacea)

Photo 6.3   Common blue violet.

Photo 6.4   Common blue violet (close-up of flower).

▼ Common Blue Violet
(continued)

General Description
- **Perennial**
- Low-growing, forming a dense colony (photo 6.3)
- Leaves emerge from a **crown** and are smooth and heart-shaped with rounded teeth along the margin
- **Petioles** are very long (two times greater than the leaf surface)
- Violetlike flowers, usually deep purple or blue, are produced on long, leafless stalks (photo 6.4)

Reproduction
- Stout, branching **rhizomes** or seeds

Location
- In turfgrass, landscapes, damp woods, road-sides, and meadows
- Often found in cemeteries
- Prefers moist, cool, shady areas

▼ Creeping or Slender Speedwell
(Veronica filiformis)

New York State Turfgrass Association

Photo 6.5   Creeping or slender speedwell.

General Description

- Prostrate, creeping **perennial**
- Resembles ground ivy but with round stems
- Leaves on vegetative stems are **opposite**, and leaves on flowering stems are **alternate**
- Stems will root at **nodes** where **stolons** touch the ground
- Small light blue to purple flowers are produced in the late spring to early summer (photo 6.5)

▼ Creeping or Slender Speedwell
(continued)

Reproduction
- Vegetative
- Stem bits that have at least a single node for rooting can be spread by mowing and **clippings**

Location
- Lawns, golf courses, parks
- Weed prefers shady, moist, cool conditions

▼ Dandelion *(Taraxacum officinale)*

Photo 6.6   Dandelion.

Photo 6.7   Dandelion seedheads.

▼ Dandelion
(continued)

General Description
- **Perennial**
- Large, **basal rosette** with long, narrow, deeply notched leaves growing from plant base (photo 6.6)
- Long, thick, fleshy **taproot**
- Bright yellow, composite flowers produced on hollow, leafless stalks
- Flowers produced from May to June and again in the fall when the day length is under 12 hours
- Flower stalks, leaves, and taproot exude a milky sap when cut
- Interesting round, puffy seedhead with easily dislodged seeds (photo 6.7)

Reproduction
- Mainly by windblown seed; occasionally develops from broken segments of taproot

Location
- In turfgrass, pastures, roadsides, orchards, gardens, waste areas, and fallow and **cultivated** fields

▼ Ground Ivy *(Glechoma hederacea)*

Photo 6.8   Ground ivy.

Photo 6.9   Ground ivy (close-up of leaf).

▼ Ground Ivy
(continued)

Rossi

Photo 6.10   Ground ivy (runner).

General Description
- Creeping **perennial**
- In the mint family
- Long, smooth, square stems that root at the **nodes**
- Leaves are small; **opposite**; kidney-shaped, round, or heart-shaped with round-toothed edges (photos 6.8 and 6.9)
- Small, funnel-shaped, pinkish purple flowers are produced in the **axillary** clusters

Reproduction
- Primarily by creeping stems that root at the nodes (photo 6.10)

Location
- In turfgrass, landscapes, roadsides, gardens, woods, orchards, and waste places
- Commonly found in rich, damp, shaded areas

▼ Hawkweed *(Hieracium* species)

Photo 6.11   Hawkweed.
Note basal rosette.

Photo 6.12   Flowering hawkweed.
Note bright orange flowers.

▼ Hawkweed
(continued)

General Description
- **Perennial**
- Prostrate **basal rosette** with **rhizomes** and **stolons** (photo 6.11)
- Leaves are slender, long, and hairy
- Small yellow or orange flowers are produced June through early July (photo 6.12)

Reproduction
- Seed, stolons, and rhizomes

Location
- Low-maintenance turfgrass areas
- Can grow in poor, dry, gravelly soils

▼ Mouse-Ear Chickweed
(Cerastium vulgatum)

Photo 6.13   Mouse-ear chickweed.
Note opposite hairy leaves (arrow).

General Description
- **Perennial**
- Stems root at the **nodes**, forming a dense mat
- Leaves are oblong, dull green, and covered with hairs (photo 6.13)
- Small, white, five-petaled flowers produced May through October

Reproduction
- Seed

Location
- Turfgrass weed that will tolerate low mowing heights and shade

▼ Red or Sheep Sorrel
(Rumex acetosella)

Photo 6.14   Red or sheep sorrel.
Note arrowhead-shaped leaf (arrow).

General Description

- **Perennial** with leaves forming from a **basal rosette**
- Young leaves are oval; mature leaves are arrowhead-shaped with two basal **lobes** (photo 6.14)
- Extensive roots and **rhizomes**
- Male (yellow-green) and female (red-brown) flowers are produced on separate plants May through September

Reproduction

- Seed and rhizomes

Location

- Often found in turfgrass with a low **pH**, poor drainage, and low fertility

▼ White Clover
(Trifolium repens)

Photo 6.15   White clover.
Note white corona (arrow).

General Description
- **Perennial**
- Three leaflets per leaf
- White "corona" present on leaf (photo 6.15)
- White flowers present
- Stems root at the **nodes**, forming a mat

Reproduction
- Seeds and **stolons**

Location
- Areas with low nitrogen (N) levels
- Prevalent in droughty areas
- Tolerates close mowing

▼ Yellow Woodsorrel
(Oxalis stricta)

Photo 6.16 Yellow woodsorrel. Note heart-shaped leaflets (arrow).

General Description
- Upright **perennial**
- Appearance is similar to black medic (see page 176), birdsfoot trefoil, and some clovers
- **Compound** leaf with three heart-shaped leaflets that can fold at midday and evening (photo 6.16)
- Margins of leaves and stems are hairy
- Produces small, bright yellow flowers May to September

Reproduction
- Seed and **rhizomes**

Location
- In **turf**, on disturbed sites such as roadsides, and at the edge of woodlands
- Will tolerate a wide range of soil and environmental conditions

Perennial, Grasses or Grasslike

▼ Annual Bluegrass *(Poa annua)*

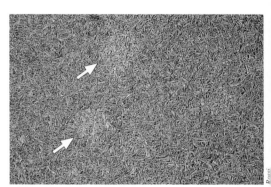

Photo 6.17   Annual bluegrass in tufts.
Note tufts (arrows).

Photo 6.18   Annual bluegrass seedheads (arrow).

▼ Annual Bluegrass
(continued)

General Description
- **Winter annual** or short-lived **perennial**
- Grows erect (to 1 foot) and forms a tight clump (photo 6.17)
- Leaf **blades** are light green, narrow, and short with parallel, wavy, or wrinkled edges and curved, boat-shaped tips
- Root system is shallow and fibrous and dies when heat- or moisture-stressed
- **Sheaths** are smooth, slightly compressed, and **keeled**; **ligules** are membranous and slightly pointed; no **auricles** are present
- **Inflorescence** is an open **panicle** with pyramidal spikes that range in color from greenish white to pinkish white (photo 6.18)

Reproduction
- Self-seeding
- Germinates in late summer or early fall, especially under cool, moist conditions

Location
- In **turf** (especially golf courses), landscapes, and gardens

▼ Nimblewill
(Muhlenbergia schreberi)

Photo 6.19   Nimblewill.

General Description

- **Perennial**
- Creeping, mat-forming grayish blue grass (photo 6.19)
- Stems are very slender and wiry
- Leaf **blades** are flat, short, and loosely spreading with hairs at the **collar** region near the leaf edge
- **Sheaths** are smooth and loosely **appressed** to the stem; **ligules** are membranous and very short; no **auricles** are present

▼ Nimblewill
(continued)

- Fine, fibrous root system is produced by **stolons** at the **nodes**

- During winter, it turns brown, but stolons persist and resprout in the spring

- **Inflorescence** is a single, very fine, slender spikelike **panicle** produced at **terminal** and **axil nodes**; spikelets are 2 millimeters long with a delicate protruding **awn**

Reproduction
- Seeds and stolons

Location
- In shady **turf**, nurseries, lawns, waste areas, thickets, pastures, and damp wooded areas

- Favors shaded areas with moist, rich soil

▼ Quackgrass *(Agropyron repens)*

Photo 6.20   Quackgrass.

Photo 6.21   Quackgrass rhizome.
Quackgrass has strong rhizomes (arrow).

▼ Quackgrass
(continued)

General Description

- **Perennial**

- Erect-growing (to 4 feet high), narrow-leafed, very aggressive grass with extensive underground **rhizomes** (photo 6.20)

- Stems are tall, light green, smooth, tufted or mat-forming, and occasionally curved at the base

- Leaf **blades** are ribbed and rough on the upper surface with an apparent **midvein** on the underside

- **Sheaths** are slightly hairy to smooth; **ligules** are short and finely toothed; and **auricles** are clawlike and clasp the stem

- **Inflorescence** is a single, thin spike with long spikelets (four- to six-seeded) arranged in two rows along the axis

Reproduction

- Seeds and multiple, thick rhizomes (photo 6.21)

Location

- In **turf**, nurseries, landscapes, gardens, pastures, and waste areas

▼ Yellow Nutsedge
(Cyperus esculentus)

Photo 6.22   Yellow nutsedge.

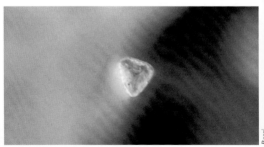

Photo 6.23   Yellow nutsedge (close-up).
Note distinct three-angled, triangular stem.

▼ Yellow Nutsedge
(continued)

General Description
- **Perennial**
- Grasslike
- Basal leaves are glossy, narrow, yellowish green in color, and formed in groups of three (photo 6.22)
- Distinct three-angled, triangular stem (photo 6.23)
- Flowers emerge as clusters of yellow to brown flattened spikelets at right angles to the stalk

Reproduction
- Primarily produced by **tubers** located at the tips of scaly **rhizomes**
- Viable seeds are also produced

Location
- In **turf**, landscapes, roadsides, gardens, and waste places
- Favors sandy soils and damp to wet low areas

Annual, Winter

▼ Annual Bluegrass
(Poa annua)

See page 160.

▼ Common Chickweed
(Stellaria media)

Photo 6.24   Common chickweed.
Note opposite glabrous leaves (arrow).

▼ Common Chickweed
(continued)

Photo 6.25   Common chickweed (close-up).

General Description

- **Winter annual** that forms dense, prostrate patches (photo 6.24)
- **Opposite**, round, shiny, **glabrous**, bright green leaves
- Fibrous, shallow roots
- Small, white, five-petaled flowers bloom from spring until fall (photo 6.25)

Reproduction

- Seed

Location

- Thrives in moist, shady soils
- Tolerates close and frequent mowing

▼ Corn Speedwell
(Veronica arvensis)

Photo 6.26   Corn speedwell.

Photo 6.27
Corn speedwell
(close-up).

▼ Corn Speedwell
(continued)

General Description
- **Winter annual** with weak but climbing stems that radiate from the base (photo 6.26)
- Lower leaves on the plants are **opposite**; upper leaves are smaller and **alternate**
- Entire plant is covered with fine hairs
- Small solitary flowers, pale blue to white, are produced in spring and summer (photo 6.27)

Reproduction
- Seed

Location
- Shaded lawns
- Dry, rocky, sandy soils

▼ Henbit *(Lamium amplexicaule)*

Photo 6.28 Henbit. Note opposite leaf (arrow).

General Description

- **Winter annual**

- Often confused with purple deadnettle

- Stem is square, green to purple, smooth or nearly hairless, and prostrate or curved at the base with ascending tips (photo 6.28)

- All leaves are **opposite** and prominently veined with soft hairs on top and deeply rounded **lobes**

▼ Henbit
(continued)

- Upper leaves encircle the stem at the base, appear **whorled**
- Lower leaves on long **petioles** are rounded to heart-shaped
- Flowers are trumpet-shaped, pink to purple, grouped in clusters of six to ten, and in whorls in the **axils** of the upper leaves
- Roots at the lower **nodes** where the stem contacts the soil surface

Reproduction
- Seed

Location
- In **turf**, landscapes, orchards, nurseries, gardens, pastures, meadows, roadsides, and waste areas
- Thrives on cool, rich, fertile soils in early spring and fall

▼ Barnyardgrass
(Echinochloa crus-galli)

Photo 6.29
Barnyard-
grass.

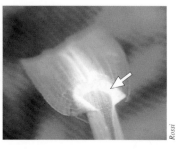

Photo 6.30
Barnyard-
grass
(close-up).
Note glabrous
collar (arrow).

▼ Barnyardgrass
(continued)

General Description

- **Summer annual**

- Semiprostrate grass producing a thick, matlike rosette, especially when growing in **turf**

- Erect-growing stems form a thick clump, branched at the **nodes** and generally bent upright (photo 6.29)

- Leaf **blades** are wide and smooth with a wavy margin and a distinct white **midvein**

- **Sheaths** are essentially closed and there are no **ligules** or **auricles**; **collar** is glabrous (photo 6.30)

- **Inflorescence** is a green to purplish **panicle** that is coarsely branched with bristled spike-lets arranged along one side of each branch of the cluster

- Drought hardy

Reproduction

- Seed only

Location

- In turf, landscapes, nurseries, roadside ditches, mudflats around ponds, and waste areas

- Commonly found in moist, rich soils

▼ Black Medic
(Medicago lupulina)

Rossi

Photo 6.31   Black medic.
Note seed (top arrow) and elongated stem on middle leaflet
(bottom arrow).

▼ Black Medic
(continued)

General Description

- Prostrate-growing **summer annual**

- Similar appearance to yellow woodsorrel (page 159), birdsfoot trefoil, and some clovers

- **Compound** leaf with three egg-shaped leaflets that have toothed margins and a point at the tip

- Center leaflet is on a longer stem than the other two leaflets (photo 6.31)

- Plants have a **taproot** and creeping stems that do not root at the **nodes**

- Clusters of small yellow flowers produced from May to September

Reproduction

- Seed (photo 6.31)

Location

- Found in nutrient-poor and drought-prone **turf** areas and disturbed areas

▼ Goosegrass *(Eleusine indica)*

Senesac

Photo 6.32   Goosegrass.
Note flattened stem (arrow).

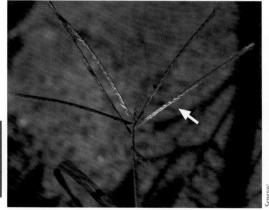

Senesac

Photo 6.33   Goosegrass seedhead.
Note zipperlike seedhead (arrow).

▼ Goosegrass
(continued)

General Description
- **Summer annual**
- Prostrate, flattened rosette with stems generally radiating outward from a central point; may also grow erect (photo 6.32)
- Sometimes confused with crabgrass, except it grows only in tufts
- Leaf **sheaths** are smooth and silvery white at the base
- Leaf **blades** are pale green and flat
- Seedhead consists of two to six spikes in clusters with flattened spikelets arranged in two rows along each spike (appears zipperlike) (photo 6.33)
- Sheaths are overlapping with long hairs along the margin; **ligules** are short and unevenly toothed; no **auricles** are present

Reproduction
- Seed only
- Germinates in warm soil temperatures above 65°F (18°C)

Location
- In **turf**, nurseries, landscapes, gardens, roadsides, waste areas, and pastures
- Droughty areas, compacted soils, or areas of close mowing

▼ Knotweed
(Polygonum aviculare)

Photo 6.34 Knotweed.
Compacted area with knotweed (arrow).

**Photo 6.35
Knotweed
(close-up).**
Note ocrea
(arrow).

▼ Knotweed
(continued)

General Description

- **Summer annual**

- Persistent weed with prostrate to ascending, branching stems that are longitudinally ridged and swollen at the joints (photo 6.34)

- Leaves are bluish green, **alternate**, oblong, and narrowed at the base

- Each **node** is covered with a thin, papery, membranous **sheath** (**ocrea**) surrounding the stem at the leaf base (photo 6.35)

- Small, inconspicuous flowers are produced in groups of one to five in **axillary** clusters; flowers are white to green with pinkish margins

- Among the first summer annual weeds to emerge in the spring

Reproduction

- Seed

Location

- In turfgrass, landscapes, waste areas, and pathways

- Thrives on hard, compacted soil, especially in high-traffic areas (photo 6.34)

▼ Large Crabgrass
(Digitaria sanguinalis)

Photo 6.36   Large crabgrass seedlings.

**Photo 6.37
Large
crabgrass.**
Note hairs
(arrow).

Turfgrass Problems: Picture Clues and Management Options

▼ Large Crabgrass
(continued)

General Description
- **Summer annual**
- Seedling leaves are hairy (photo 6.36)
- Growth pattern is usually prostrate and spreading, but growth can be ascending (up to 3 feet)
- Prostrate, smooth, elongated stems commonly root at the **nodes**
- Leaf **blades** are wide with a prominent **midvein** and stiff hairs on both surfaces at a 90° angle to the plant surface (photo 6.37)
- **Sheath** is greenish red with long, stiff hairs; no **auricles**; and a white, membranous, jagged **ligule**
- **Inflorescence** consists of two to ten long, fingerlike spikes in clusters radiating from a central point at the top of the stem

Reproduction
- Seed and rooting stems at nodes

Location
- In **turf**, landscapes, gardens, pastures, and waste areas

▼ Prostrate Spurge
(Euphorbia supina)

Photo 6.38   Prostrate spurge.
Note purple spot on leaf (arrow).

General Description

- **Summer annual**
- Prone growth habit forms a flat, dense mat
- Mature leaves are **opposite** and oblong with a purplish blotch in the center (photo 6.38)
- Pinkish, hairy stems exude white sap when injured or broken
- Small, whitish pink flowers are produced July through September

Reproduction

- Seed

Location

- Dry, sandy soil
- Disturbed and compacted soils

▼ Smooth Crabgrass
(Digitaria ischaemum)

Photo 6.39   Smooth crabgrass.

Photo 6.40   Smooth crabgrass.
Note patch of light-colored crabgrass in middle of photo.

Smooth Crabgrass continued on page 186 ▶

Weeds

185

▼ Smooth Crabgrass
(continued)

Photo 6.41 Smooth crabgrass seedheads. Note fingerlike seedheads.

DiTomaso

▼ Smooth Crabgrass
(continued)

General Description

- **Summer annual**
- Similar to large crabgrass, except it has smooth stems, **sheaths**, and leaf **blades** and is generally smaller (photos 6.39 and 6.40, page 185)
- Leaf blades are narrow and prostrate with hairs only in the **collar** region
- Stems branch at **nodes**, but no rooting occurs at nodes
- **Inflorescence** consists of two to six slender, fingerlike clusters of spikes not radiating from a single point (photo 6.41)

Reproduction

- Seed only

Location

- In **turf**, landscapes, gardens, pastures, and waste areas

Glossary

Abiotic Nonliving

Acervulus (plural, acervuli) Asexual, saucer-shaped reproductive fungal structures

Acidic Having a pH less than 7

Aerate Loosen by mechanical means to allow air to enter; spiked rollers are used to aerate lawns

Alkaline Having a pH greater than 7

Alternate (leaves) Arranged singly along an axis, one leaf per node

Anaerobic Occurring in the absence of oxygen

Annual See **Summer annual** and **Winter annual**

Appressed Pressed closely and flatly against

Auricle A small, projecting lobe or appendage on grass leaves, found at the juncture of the leaf blade and the leaf sheath

Awn A sharp point or bristle found at the tip of a grass seed or grain

Axil The area where a leaf or flower stem and stem join

Axillary Occurring at the axil

Basal rosette A circular cluster of leaves radiating from the stem of a plant at ground level

Basidiomycete A group of fungi characterized by the production of spores on a club-shaped filament called the basidium

Biennial A plant that requires two growing seasons to complete its life cycle; vegetative growth occurs in year one, followed by seedhead formation in year two

Biotic Living

Blade The expanded, flattened part of a leaf or petal

Blight The rapid killing of leaves and stems from a single point of infection

Bunch grass A grass without stolons or rhizomes; has a growth habit of forming a bunch

Castings, earthworm The roundish fecal pellets of earthworms that are deposited on the surface around a tunneling or burrow

Chlorosis An abnormal condition in the plant stem and leaves where the synthesis of the green pigment (chlorophyll) is inhibited, resulting in a pale yellow color

Chlorotic Having chlorosis

Clippings Leaves and stems cut off by mowing

Collar The juncture of the leaf blade and sheath

Compaction A physical condition of the soil resulting from the compression of the soil particles into a dense mass; common around sidewalks, roadways, and heavily trafficked areas

Compost Organic material (such as plant remains or manure) broken down by microorganisms to a relatively stable intermediate stage; compost is used as a soil conditioner

Compound leaf A leaf that is made up of two or more leaflets

Cool-season turfgrass A grass species adapted to favorable growth during the cooler portions of the growing season, when temperatures are 60°–75°F (16°–24°C); the principal species of cool-season turfgrasses are creeping bentgrasses, colonial bentgrasses, Kentucky bluegrasses, annual bluegrasses, fine-leaf fescues, tall fescues, and perennial ryegrasses

Core cultivation A type of aeration in which a hollow- or solid-tined unit is used to improve soil texture and manage thatch

Crown The growing point of a perennial plant at or below the ground where the root and stem join and new shoots are produced

Cultivar A cultivated variety; a group of plants with distinguishing characteristics that are preserved by some means of controlled propagation

Cultivation Loosening or breaking up of the soil around plants

Cup cutter A boring tool that cuts and cleanly removes a cylindrical core of soil 4.25 inches across

Desiccate To dry

Dew Water droplets that condense from the air

Dormancy The state of temporary growth cessation and a general slowing down of other activities

Endophyte Fungi that grow inside certain grasses; they produce compounds that are toxic to some surface-feeding insects and can increase drought and heat tolerance

Foliar Pertaining to the leaves

Fungus (plural, fungi) An organism that lacks chlorophyll and cannot make its own food; included are molds, yeasts, smuts, and mushrooms

Glabrous Smooth; having a surface without hairs or projections

Growing degree days (GDD) A measure of accumulated heat units relative to a predetermined base temperature; a temperature degree of deviation from a single day's mean temperature; GDD can influence plant and pest development; see pages 10–11 for more information

Grub An immature insect that lives in the soil, resembles a milky white worm or caterpillar, and feeds on plant roots

Herbicide A chemical used to control weeds

Host The plant on or in which an organism lives and from which it feeds

Humidity Water vapor that is in the air

Hydrophobic Lacking an affinity for water; water-repellant

Inflorescence The flowering portion of a shoot

Instar The growth stages of some insects in between molts

Integrated pest management (IPM) An approach to the management of pests in which all available control options, including physical, biological, and chemical controls, are evaluated and integrated into a unified program; seeks to minimize the disruption of natural mortality factors and maintain a healthy plant

IPM See **Integrated pest management (IPM)**

Keel Central ridge on the back or outer surface of a folded leaf or seed

Larva (plural, larvae) A young insect that does not resemble the adult

Leach To apply water in excess of the amount retained by the soil to promote drainage of excess salts and fertilizer residues from the root zone

Leaf blade The upper part of the grass leaf

Leaf sheath The lower portion of the grass leaf that is attached to the grass crown

Lesion A localized area of diseased plant tissue; a wound

Ligule A hairy or membranous appendage located where the leaf blade meets the leaf sheath

Lobe A division or segment of a leaf, usually rounded in outline, that extends to the central vein of the leaf

Lodging Falling over due to wind or rain

Midvein The central vein of a leaf

Mycelium (plural, mycelia) Fungal threads that make up the body of the fungus

Node A place on a stem where a leaf is or was attached

Nymph A young insect that resembles the adult minus the wings

Ocrea A papery sheath that encloses the stem at the nodes

Opposite (leaves) Two leaves at the same level on opposite sides of a stem or other axis; two leaves per node

Organic fertilizer Fertilizers derived from living organisms

Panicle An inflorescence that has a main axis and subdivided branches; may be compact and spikelike

Pathogen An agent that causes disease

Perennial A plant that has a life span of more than two years

Perithecium (plural, perithecia) Sexual reproductive fungal structure

Petiole The stalk of a leaf

pH A measure of the acidity (pH less than 7) or alkalinity (pH greater than 7) of a solution; a pH of 7 is neutral; pH is known to influence nutrient availability

Pheromone A chemical produced for communication among the members of insect species; the most well-known examples are sex pheromones, which are used by one sex to attract the other for mating

Photosynthesis The plant process where energy from sunlight converts carbon dioxide (CO_2) and water into carbohydrates used by the plant as food

Physical amendment Substance added to soil to alter the physical condition of the soil; examples are sand, peat moss, and lime

Pustule A small, often distinctively colored elevation or spot resembling a blister

Raster pattern A pattern composed of bare spaces, hairs, and spines on the anus of certain white grubs

Relative humidity The amount of water vapor in the air, compared to the amount the air could hold if it were totally saturated; expressed as a percentage

Renovation Partial or entire replanting of a site

Rhizomatous Having rhizomes

Rhizome An underground stem

Runner See **Stolon**

Scape A leafless flower stalk arising from the underground or subsurface parts of a plant

Scarab Common name for any of various large, bright-colored beetles of which about 30,000 are found worldwide

Sclerotium (plural, sclerotia) Small, hard fungal structure that is capable of surviving under unfavorable environmental conditions

Scouting The process of systematically searching for pests; it is the cornerstone of any integrated pest management (IPM) program

Sheath The lower part of the grass leaf that closes around the stem

Soluble Capable of being dissolved

Spore The asexual reproductive unit of fungi

Stand A group of plants growing in an area

Stolon A horizontal stem at or above the ground

Stoloniferous Having stolons

Summer annual Plant whose seeds germinate in the spring, grow through the summer, flower, produce seed, and die in the fall

Syringe To spray turf with small amounts of water in order to cool it, prevent or correct wilt, or remove frost or dew

Taproot A large, vertical root such as a carrot

Terminal node A node at the tip of a stem

Thatch The layer of decomposed or partially decomposed organic material between the green part of the plant and the soil; small amounts may be beneficial to insulate the soil, cushion the surface, and support an active microbial population

Threshold The number or level of a pest that can be tolerated or accepted before applying control measures

Tiller A shoot growing from the base (crown) of a grass plant

Topdress The act of applying topdressing

Topdressing Soil mix added to the surface of the turf and worked in by brooming, raking, and irrigation

Tuber A swollen, usually underground stem that stores food for the plant; a potato is an example

Turf A turfgrass plant, the thatch, and the roots growing with the soil

Ventral Of or relating to the belly; abdominal

Wetting agent A material used to improve wettability by reducing surface tension

Whorled Having three or more leaves per node

Winter annual A plant that germinates in the late fall to early spring, produces seed in spring, and then dies

Witches' broom A dense, bushy growth of branches and foliage caused by a parasitic fungus and mites or poor pruning techniques

Conversion Factors

▼ LENGTH

Equivalents
1 foot (ft) = 12 inches (in)
1 yard (yd) = 3 ft
1 mile (mi) = 1,760 yd

1 centimeter (cm) = 10 millimeters (mm)
1 meter (m) = 100 cm
1 kilometer (km) = 1,000 m

Conversions
1 in = 2.54 cm
1 ft = 0.305 m
1 mi = 1.61 km

▼ AREA

Equivalents
1 square foot (ft^2) = 144 square inches (in^2)
1 square yard (yd^2) = 9 ft^2
1 acre (ac) = 4,840 yd^2
1 square mile (mi^2) = 640 ac

1 square meter (m^2) = 10,000 square centimeters (cm^2)
1 hectare (ha) = 10,000 m^2
1 square kilometer (km^2) = 1,000,000 m^2

Conversions
1 in^2 = 6.45 cm^2
1 ft^2 = 0.093 m^2
1 ac = 0.405 ha
1 mi^2 = 2.59 km^2

▼ VOLUME

Equivalents

1 tablespoon (Tbsp) = 3 teaspoons (tsp)
1 cup = 8 fluid ounces (fl oz)
1 quart (qt) = 2 pints (pt) = 4 cups
1 gallon (gal) = 4 qt = 231 cubic inches (in^3)

1 milliliter (ml) = 1,000 microliters (μl)
1 liter (L) = 1,000 ml = 1,000 cubic centimeters (cm^3 or cc)
1 cm^3 = 1 ml

Conversions

1 tsp = 4.93 ml
1 fl oz = 29.6 ml
1 qt = 0.946 L
1 gal = 3.785 L
1 in^3 = 16.387 cm^3

▼ MASS OR WEIGHT

Equivalents

1 pound (lb) = 16 ounces (oz)
1 ton = 2,000 lb

1 gram (g) = 1,000 milligrams (mg)
1 kilogram (kg) = 1,000 g
1 metric ton (mt) = 1,000 kg

Conversions

1 oz = 28.35 g
1 lb = 0.454 kg
1 ton = 0.907 mt

▼ TEMPERATURE

$$°F = (°C \times \tfrac{9}{5}) + 32$$
$$°C = (°F - 32) \times \tfrac{5}{9}$$

References

Baxendale, F. P., and R. E. Gaussoin, eds. 1997. *Integrated Turfgrass Management for the Northern Great Plains.* Lincoln, NE: University of Nebraska.

Brandenburg, R. L., and M. G. Villani, eds. 1995. *Handbook of Turfgrass Insect Pests.* Lanham, MD: Entomological Society of America.

Burpee, L. L. 1993. *A Guide to Integrated Control of Turfgrass Diseases.* Volume I, *Cool-Season Turfgrasses.* Lawrence, KS: Golf Course Superintendents Association of America Press.

Couch, H. B. 1995. *Diseases of Turfgrasses.* 3rd ed. Malabar, FL: Krieger Publishing.

Dernoeden, P. H., and N. Jackson, eds. 1995. *Diseases of Turfgrasses.* Greensboro, NC: Ciba-Geigy Corporation.

Petrovic, A. Martin, Maria T. Cinque, Richard W. Smiley, and Haruo Tashiro. 1982. *Picture Clues to Turfgrass Problems.* Ithaca, NY: Cornell Cooperative Extension.

Schumann, G. L., P. J. Vittum, M. L. Elliott, and P. P. Cobb. 1998. *IPM Handbook for Golf Courses.* Chelsea, MI: Ann Arbor Press.

Shetlar, D. J., P. R. Heller, and P. D. Irish. 1990. *Turfgrass Insect and Mite Manual.* 3rd ed. Bellefonte, PA: Pennsylvania Turfgrass Council.

Smiley, R. W., P. H. Dernoeden, and B. B. Clarke. 1993. *Compendium of Turfgrass Diseases.* 2nd ed. St. Paul, MN: American Phytopathological Society Press.

Smith, J. D., N. Jackson, and A. R. Woolhouse. 1989. *Fungal Diseases of Amenity Turf Grasses*. 3rd ed. London: E & FN Spon.

TruGreen – ChemLawn. 1994. *Turf Field Guide*. Delaware, OH: ChemLawn Corporation.

Uva, R. H., J. C. Neal, and J. M. DiTomaso. 1997. *Weeds of the Northeast*. Ithaca, NY: Cornell University Press.

Watschke, Thomas L., Peter H. Dernoeden, and David J. Shetlar. 1995. *Managing Turfgrass Pests*. Boca Raton, FL: Lewis Publishers.

Peer Reviewers

Dr. Steven R. Alm, Professor of Entomology, Department of Plant Sciences, University of Rhode Island

Nancy F. Bosold, Extension Agent–Turfgrass Management, Berks County Cooperative Extension, The Pennsylvania State University

Sid Bosworth, Extension Associate Professor, Department of Plant and Soil Science, University of Vermont

David R. Chalmers, Associate Professor and Extension Agronomist–Turfgrass Management, Department of Crop and Soil Environmental Sciences, Virginia Polytechnic Institute and State University

Bruce B. Clarke, Extension Specialist–Turfgrass Pathology, Department of Plant Pathology, Rutgers University

Peter H. Dernoeden, Professor of Agronomy, Department of Natural Resource Sciences and Landscape Architecture, University of Maryland–College Park

William M. Dest, Associate Professor Emeritus, Department of Plant Science, University of Connecticut

J. Scott Ebdon, Assistant Professor–Turfgrass Science, Department of Plant and Soil Sciences, University of Massachusetts

Scott D. Guiser, Extension Agent, Bucks County Cooperative Extension, The Pennsylvania State University

George W. Hamilton, Jr., Senior Lecturer of Turfgrass Science, Department of Agronomy, The Pennsylvania State University

Robert E. Leiby, County Extension Director, Lehigh County Cooperative Extension, The Pennsylvania State University

Edwin E. Lewis, Assistant Professor, Department of Entomology, Virginia Polytechnic Institute and State University

John M. Roberts, Extension Turf Specialist, Department of Plant Biology, University of New Hampshire

John E. Rowehl, Cooperative Extension Agent, Cumberland County Cooperative Extension, The Pennsylvania State University

Bridget A. Ruemmele, Associate Professor–Turfgrass Improvement, Department of Plant Sciences, University of Rhode Island

Jude Serevino, Master Gardener, Prince William County, Virginia

A. J. Turgeon, Professor of Turfgrass Management, Department of Agronomy, The Pennsylvania State University

Michael G. Villani, Professor of Soil Insect Ecology and Turf Entomology, New York State Agricultural Experiment Station, Cornell University

Jim Welshans, Extension Agent–Turfgrass, Capital Region Cooperative Extension, The Pennsylvania State University

Photo Credits

Individuals

Liz Davis Clark

Peter H. Dernoeden, Professor of Agronomy, Department of Natural Resource Sciences and Landscape Architecture, University of Maryland–College Park

Jeffrey F. Derr, Professor of Weed Science, Hampton Roads Agricultural Research and Extension Center, Virginia Polytechnic Institute and State University

Joseph M. DiTomaso, Extension Noncrop Weed Ecologist, Weed Science Program, University of California–Davis

Peter J. Landschoot, Associate Professor of Turfgrass Science, Department of Agronomy, The Pennsylvania State University

David P. LoParco, Research Technician, Department of Plant Pathology, Cornell University

Joseph C. Neal, Professor and Extension Specialist–Weed Science, Department of Horticultural Science, North Carolina State University

Andrew F. Senesac, Extension Educator–Weed Science, Long Island Horticultural Research and Extension Center, Cornell Cooperative Extension

James E. Skorulski, Agronomist, United States Golf Association

Richard H. Uva, Ph.D. Candidate, Department of Horticulture, Cornell University

Joseph M. Vargas, Jr., Professor, Department of Botany and Plant Pathology, Michigan State University

Universities and Others

The American Phytopathological Society, < WWW.APSNET.ORG > (Photos were reprinted, with permission, from *Compendium of Turfgrass Diseases,* 2nd Edition, 1992, The American Phytopathological Society, St. Paul, Minnesota.)

Cornell University, Plant Disease Diagnostic Clinic

CRC Press, Inc. (Photos were reprinted, with permission, from J. M. Vargas, Jr., *Management of Turfgrass Diseases,* 2nd Edition, 1994, CRC Press, Inc., Boca Raton, Florida.)

New York State Agricultural Experiment Station (NYSAES), Cornell University, Geneva, New York (Photos are from Dr. Michael Villani's collection of turfgrass photos and are reproduced with permission from Dr. Michael Villani and NYSAES.)

New York State Turfgrass Association, Latham, New York, < WWW.NYSTA.ORG >

The Pennsylvania State University, Department of Agronomy

University of Nebraska–Lincoln, Turfgrass Science Team

About the Authors

Eva Gussack is an Extension Associate in the Department of Horticulture at Cornell University. She works in turfgrass with Dr. Frank S. Rossi. She obtained her Bachelor of Science degree in 1995 and Master of Science degree in 1997, both from Cornell University. Prior to returning to school, she owned and operated a successful interior and exterior landscaping business in New York City for over ten years, servicing residential and corporate clientele.

Eva works with Frank to produce the award-winning weekly newsletter *ShortCUTT*, which is now in its third season of publication, and coauthored with Frank the recently published *Homeowner's Lawn Care and Water Quality Almanac*, an easy-to-use, twelve-step program to preserve water quality. Eva and Frank are currently

awaiting a patent for removable sports turf paint that addresses multi-use athletic fields.

Dr. Frank S. Rossi, Extension Turfgrass Specialist and Assistant Professor of Turfgrass Management in the Department of Horticulture at Cornell University, has been a member of the turfgrass industry for over two decades. He has served on the faculties at Michigan State University and University of Wisconsin–Madison and has worked to develop programs that focus on resource-efficient, sustainable turfgrass management. Frank has advised major industry associations—including the Golf Course Superintendents Association of America (GCSAA), Professional Lawn Care Association of America (PLCAA), and United States Golf Association (USGA).

Frank was recently named one of the top forty most influential people in the golf industry under the age of forty by *Golfweek* magazine, an achievement he shares with folks like Tiger Woods and Jack Nicklaus III. He was twice a recipient of a Certificate of Excellence from the American Society of Agronomy—in 1998 for the video *Low-Input Lawn Care* and again in 1996 as editor of the quarterly newsletter *Cornell University Turfgrass Times (CUTT)*.

About NRAES

NRAES, the Natural Resource, Agriculture, and Engineering Service, is a not-for-profit program dedicated to assisting land grant university faculty and others in increasing the public availability of research- and experience-based knowledge. NRAES is sponsored by fourteen land grant universities in the eastern United States (see map on page 208). We receive administrative support from Cornell University, the host university.

When you buy books from NRAES, you are helping to improve the accessibility of land grant university knowledge. While 15% of NRAES' annual income is provided by member universities, the funds to publish new books and coordinate new conferences come from our customers through book sales, conference registrations, and occasional project-specific grants.

NRAES publishes practical books of interest to fruit and vegetable growers, landscapers, dairy and livestock producers, natural resource managers, SWCD (soil and water conservation district) staff, consumers, landowners, and professionals interested in agricultural waste management and composting. NRAES books are used in cooperative extension programs, in college courses, as management guides, and for self-directed learning.

NRAES publishes two types of books: peer-reviewed books and conference proceedings. NRAES also distributes some videos. Contact us (see page 208) for more information or a free book catalog.

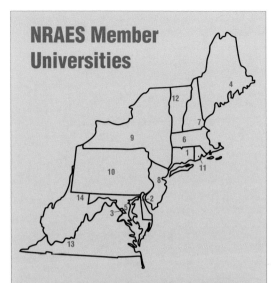

NRAES Member Universities

1. University of Connecticut • 2. University of Delaware • 3. University of the District of Columbia • 4. University of Maine • 5. University of Maryland • 6. University of Massachusetts • 7. University of New Hampshire • 8. Rutgers University • 9. Cornell University • 10. The Pennsylvania State University • 11. University of Rhode Island • 12. University of Vermont • 13. Virginia Polytechnic Institute and State University • 14. West Virginia University

NRAES • Cooperative Extension
PO Box 4557 • Ithaca, New York 14852-4557
Phone: (607) 255-7654 • Fax: (607) 254-8770
E-mail: NRAES@CORNELL.EDU • Web site: WWW.NRAES.ORG
Office hours: Monday through Thursday, 8:30 A.M. to
4:30 P.M., and Friday, 8:30 A.M. to 2:30 P.M., eastern time

Marty Sailus, NRAES Director
Jeffrey S. Popow, NRAES Managing Editor

Other Publications of Interest

From NRAES

The publications below are available from NRAES. To order, contact NRAES for current prices and shipping and handling charges. Books can be ordered on our web site (WWW.NRAES.ORG). See page 208 for our contact information and office hours.

Greenhouses for Homeowners and Gardeners (NRAES–137)
This book covers every aspect of designing and constructing a home greenhouse—from foundations and utilities to bench design and lighting systems. Eight chapters discuss greenhouse basics, greenhouse selection, planning, framing and glazing materials, layouts and equipment, the greenhouse environment, window greenhouses and growth chambers, and garden structures. This amply illustrated book includes 10 construction plans. (2000, 214 pages)

Home*A*Syst: An Environmental Risk-Assessment Guide for the Home (NRAES–87)
Home*A*Syst helps people assess homes for pollution and health risks. Eleven chapters cover site assessment, stormwater management, drinking water well management, household wastewater, hazardous household products, lead in the home, yard and garden care, liquid fuels management, indoor air quality, heating and cooling systems, and household waste management. (1997, 122 pages)

Composting to Reduce the Waste Stream: A Guide to Small Scale Food and Yard Waste Composting (NRAES–43)

This publication promotes small-scale composting of yard, garden, and vegetative food waste. Topics covered are the composting process, composting methods, making and maintaining a compost pile, and using compost. Seventeen figures, six tables, and plans for constructing nine types of compost bins are included. (1991, 44 pages)

From Cornell Cooperative Extension

The publication below is available from the Cornell University Resource Center, 7 Business and Technology Park, Ithaca, New York 14850; phone: (607) 255-2080. The center's web site (WWW.CCE. CORNELL.EDU/PUBLICATIONS/CATALOG.HTML) contains an order form and a list of other books available from Cornell Cooperative Extension. Contact the center for current prices and shipping and handling charges.

The Homeowner's Lawn Care and Water Quality Almanac (141S2)

Put together by the authors of *Turfgrass Problems: Picture Clues and Management Options,* this spiral-bound, calendar-style almanac teaches homeowners how to grow and maintain a dense, healthy lawn without polluting watersheds. Organized as a month-by-month checklist, it includes color illustrations, charts, and recommendations to help readers decide what is best for their lawns and their environment. The almanac is easy to use and filled with unique tips and helpful ideas. At the end of the year, flip from December back to January, and the twelve-step guide to a healthy lawn and healthy environment is ready to use all over again. (2000, 28 laminated pages)